F
AFIELD

Terence Jenkins

FURTHER
AFIELD

TERENCE JENKINS

Copyright © 2013 Terence Jenkins

The moral right of the author has been asserted.

Apart from any fair dealing for the purposes of research or private study, or criticism or review, as permitted under the Copyright, Designs and Patents Act 1988, this publication may only be reproduced, stored or transmitted, in any form or by any means, with the prior permission in writing of the publishers, or in the case of reprographic reproduction in accordance with the terms of licences issued by the Copyright Licensing Agency. Enquiries concerning reproduction outside those terms should be sent to the publishers.

Matador
9 Priory Business Park
Kibworth Beauchamp
Leicestershire LE8 0RX, UK
Tel: (+44) 116 279 2299
Fax: (+44) 116 279 2277
Email: books@troubador.co.uk
Web: www.troubador.co.uk/matador

ISBN 978 1783060 283

British Library Cataloguing in Publication Data.
A catalogue record for this book is available from the British Library.

Typeset in Bembo by Troubador Publishing Ltd

Matador is an imprint of Troubador Publishing Ltd

For those who take the road less travelled

Also by Terence Jenkins:

Another Man's London
London Lives
London Tales
Return: A Collection of Short Stories
Co-Author of *The Book of Penge, Anerley and Crystal Palace*

CONTENTS

The Burial Place of the Music Makers	1
A Common Pursuit	9
A Very Rascally Piece of Earth	19
Amber	27
Amethyst	35
An Early Eco-Warrior	43
An Unsung Hero of Medicine	51
Aur Cymru: Welsh Gold	59
Cenotaphs	67
Edith	77
Fitter for An History than a Sermon	85
FitzRoy	95
He Being Dead, Yet Speaketh	105
Martyrs	115
Pink Satin Lips	123
Snotty-Gogs and Pontius Pilate	131
The Last Plantagenet?	141
The Lillie Pad	151
The Shropshire Pirate	159
They Had No Choice	167

THE BURIAL PLACE OF THE MUSIC MAKERS

THE BURIAL PLACE OF THE MUSIC MAKERS

Keep this to yourself, but I think I may be one of the Undead. No, seriously, I have this enduring fascination for churchyards and cemeteries. I don't mean that I frequent them at night and bay at the moon, but friends think me strange, morbid even, to enjoy strolling among the stiffs and reading epitaphs. I can't think where I got it from, most of my family are ordinary folk but my maternal granny did tell me once of a great-aunt, Pippi Strell, who was a little batty.

Anyway, I've done them all, the famous ones, that is. Many a jolly Sunday afternoon I've spent exploring the London ones: Highgate and Karl Marx; West Norwood with the Doultons, Tates, Maxim (of machine gun fame), Mrs Beeton (of '*Household Management*') and the splendid Greek Orthodox section with its collection of elaborate tombs; Nunhead with its ruined church and paths that weave in and out of the ever-encroaching vegetation. I've even taken my interest with me on holidays and scouted for the graves of Toscanini, Catalani, Horowitz and, for a few years, Eva Peron in the Monumental Cemetery in Milan. With hundreds of others, I've got in line and shuffled past Epstein's often attacked memorial to dear old Oscar in Pere La Chaise and, on the way, taken in Jim Morrison's final resting place though I don't think he was getting that much rest, not with the hordes who were besieging his grave. I have even clumped around a Bogomil necropolis in the Balkans. My favourite of all these has been the graveyard on the island of San Michele in the Venetian lagoon with its high brick wall all round and the tall, dark cypress trees that overshadow the paths that wind between the different sections: the Protestant section where you can find the graves of Baron Corvo (author of '*Hadrian IV*', a favourite book of mine) and Ezra Pound (not a favourite poet of mine);the Orthodox section where Serge Diaghilev and Igor Stravinsky lie beside each other and are often covered with tributes from ballet and music lovers, while forgotten Russian princesses and aristocrats share the same earth at the end of lives in exile. All very romantically melancholic. Just up my street. (If you want to go there, get on vaporetto 41 or 42 from Fondamente Nuove and get off at the first stop.) However, perhaps my most favourite of all lies much nearer than La Serenissima.

Beneath one of the highest points on the Downs (900 feet), close to the Kent border, is the Surrey village of Limpsfield. Lying on the Greenwich Meridian about 21 miles due south of London and not yet completely absorbed by ever-expanding Oxted, its neighbour, it has a wealth of attractive buildings:Georgian houses, tile-hung cottages, a village shop, a welcoming pub and a very good bookshop. Once, above the village, on Titsey Hill, there was a Roman villa and the Pilgrims' Way to Canterbury passes nearby.

Although surrounded by much else of historical interest, it is the village church, St Peters, which attracts visitors. It is

The grave of Sir Thomas Beecham, conductor and founder of The Royal Philharmonic Orchestra. He championed the work of Fredrick Delius, who is buried nearby. He is buried between Eileen Joyce, the concert pianist, and another conductor, Norman Del Mar.

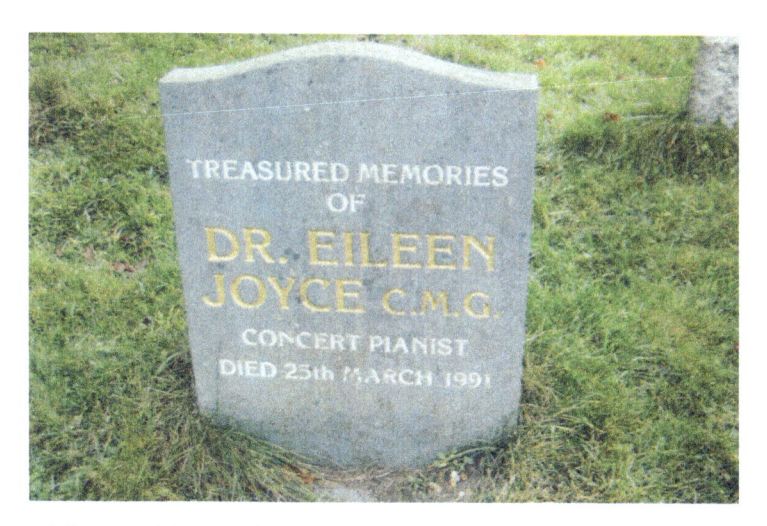

The grave of Dame Eileen Joyce C.M.G, the concert pianist and one-time inhabitant of Limpsfield, is buried in the churchyard of St Peters, next to two famous conductors – Sir Thomas Beecham and Normal Del Mar C.B.E.

The Burial Place of the Music Makers 5

a handsome building, of Norman origin and is mentioned in the Domesday Book, William the Conqueror's survey of England for tax purposes, made in 1086. It stands in a prominent position in the High Street and once belonged to Battle Abbey and, apart from the courthouse, is the only remaining building from that time.

It is the graveyard to which most visitors are drawn for there in the quiet sylvan surroundings of God's acre not only do 'the rude forefathers of the hamlet sleep' but many famous musicians are also buried.

Dr Eileen Joyce (1912-1991), the Australian concert pianist who had trained at Leipzig, is buried here. Her home was in Limpsfield and she would give concerts for locals who thronged her music gallery as she, sometimes accompanied by a protégé, would play, using two grand pianos. She also worked on film soundtracks, most famously for that of '*Brief Encounter*', a perennial favourite. Dr Joyce endeared herself to the British by her radio broadcasts during World War II and her visits to many blitzed cities and towns up and down the country.

Nearby is the grave of the prolific composer Frederick Delius (1862-1934) who worked as an orange farmer in Florida at one time. He, too, like Eileen Joyce, had studied at Leipzig and when he moved to live mainly in France, he composed choral and orchestral works, chamber music and songs as well as operas, perhaps the famous of which is '*A Village Romeo and Juliet*' with its well-known '*Walk to the Paradise Garden*'.

For the last decade of his life he was blind and paralysed from a syphilitic infection, but with the help of the musician Eric Fenby as his amanuensis, he continued to compose such

In the graveyard of the parish church of St Peter, Limpsfield, are the Harrison sisters' graves. It was Beatrice, the cellist, who made the famous first outside broadcast for the BBC when she played her cello in a wood and a nightingale sang.

works as '*A Song of Summer*' and '*Songs of Farewell*'. When he died in 1934 his wife, Jelka, had him buried him in the churchyard at Grez-sur-Loing near Fontainbleau. However, he had wished to be buried somewhere in the south of England and in May 1935, after much searching, she had his body brought to St Peter's churchyard where it now lies beneath a grey slate headstone next to his wife's grave, for she too chose this quiet rural spot as her last resting place.

One of the great champions of Delius's work was Sir Thomas Beecham, conductor and founder of the Royal Philharmonic Orchestra, who read the eulogy at Delius's funeral. When Sir Thomas died in 1961, he was buried at Brookwood cemetery, but thirty years later in 1991 his body was transferred to Limpsfield to be close to that of the man whose music and reputation he had fostered.

To the left of Sir Thomas's grave is that of Norman Del Mar who though he was a horn-player and composer, is chiefly remembered as a conductor, especially of the works of Elgar, Mahler and Richard Strauss about whom he wrote three books.

The ashes of Jack Brymer, the famous clarinettist, are buried here too. He was one of the finest clarinettists of his time and played under Sir Thomas's baton during his career.

Nearby is the grave of the Harrison sisters, all musicians. The most famous was the cellist, Beatrice, who made the first BBC outside broadcast when she played her cello in a wood where a nightingale was singing, a recording still remembered and requested by many. The sisters' headstone has inscribed on it a quote from an ode by the Victorian poet, Arthur O'Shaughnessy:

'We are the music makers

We are the dreamers of dreams'

How appropriate for a churchyard with so many music makers.

Many visitors to this part of England come to see the great country houses, Knole, Sissinghurst, Hever, Penshurst, Leeds and Scotney castles but a detour to this lovely corner of our country will repay you well. So, if you want to join the Undead in a stroll amongst the dear departed, join me.

A COMMON PURSUIT

A COMMON PURSUIT

'Let's take the dog for walk.'

'Why not? It's a sunny spring afternoon so let's venture forth with mutt.'

And off we went but this time not to one of our nearer green spaces. Be bold, I think, and go to the far reaches of Croydon, and that's how we came to be strolling on Kenley Common, 56 acres of green open space owned and managed, along with five other commons on the southern fringe of the metropolis, by the Corporation of the City of London. Kenley is part of the 10,000 acres of open spaces thus owned, along with more famous park and woodland areas such as Hampstead Heath and Burnham Beeches. Little did I know how much I was to find out about Kenley when we stopped for a postprandial pint at The Wattenden Arms, a welcoming pub.

The walls were covered with old pictures of the nearby Kenley airfield during the war.

'Must have been their local,' said my companion to a fellow toper and pointed to the photos. It was an 'Ancient Mariner' moment for, once started, the bloke couldn't stop and we got the history of RAF Kenley in technicolour. This is the potted version.

On August 19th 2000, sixty years after the Battle of Britain, on a hilltop airfield in the Surrey countryside south of London, Air Commodore Sir Anthony Bagnall unveiled the RAF Kenley tribute, a memorial 'To honour all who served here 1917-59'. The 20 tonnes of Portland stone show a pilot flanked by aircrew and records all squadrons who flew from Kenley, British, Australian, New Zealand, Canadian, American, Czech, Belgian and Polish. It is a fitting tribute to all those who contributed to our island history and world peace.

Kenley began life as an Aircraft Acceptance Park in 1917 when the First World War was at its height and the Government requisitioned Kenley Common against much local opposition. Aeroplanes destined for the squadrons in France were tested and prepared for service here. The site was ideal: it was on high ground, over 500 feet; had good road and rail connections; and, importantly, there was plenty of land to expand if needed.

Work on the aerodrome began in 1917. Soon, Bessonneau portable hangers were erected to receive such planes as SE5s, DH9s and Camels, Dolphins and Salamanders from the Sopwith factory at Kingston not far away. Belfast-type sheds were also built.

At first, the men lived under canvas but soon barrack rooms and other permanent buildings followed and No.7 Kenley Acceptance Park became fully functioning, guarded by Boer War veterans, men of the Royal Defence Corps. Parts supplied by factories were received, assembled and built into planes which were then flown south across the Channel to 'our boys' in France. By 1918, Kenley was

The RAF Kenley Tribute in Honour of All who Served Here 1917-1959

A Common Pursuit 13

playing a crucial role in the war effort: its average monthly output was 56 machines. The size of the base had increased to 844 personnel and was increased even further when America joined the war and sent some of their Air Force to train as mechanics.

By the time of the Armistice on November 11th 1918, Kenley's chief role as an Aircraft Acceptance Park had been fulfilled. If the local residents expected the return of their Common, their expectations were soon dashed for Winston Churchill (who was having flying lessons at Kenley) said, in answer to a question in the House of Commons, that the aerodrome was too important in any future defence of the capital to be returned: it would, therefore, be retained as a permanent RAF base although a small part was returned to public use.

The interwar years were not without incident at Kenley. A dirigible which set out to bombard the Houses of Parliament with suffragette leaflets was blown off course and had to land at Caterham. The pressure of national emergency having been removed, flying for enjoyment became more apparent. Friendly rivalry grew between squadrons and airfields, such as that between Kenley and Northolt, which resulted in such incidents as the 'Bumf Raid' which the Surrey airmen carried out on their Middlesex colleagues, dropping toilet rolls on them. Northolt responded by dropping a load of old boots and shoes on their Kenley rival. Goodness knows what might have been dropped next.

There were important visitors to Kenley. In May 1921, the Crown Prince of Japan, later Emperor Hirohito, watched a display of No.24 Squadron. Later the same year, the Emir of Katsina was taken up for a demonstration flight. Perhaps the most famous visitor was a fellow airman, the young American Charles Lindbergh, who, in 1927, fresh from his solo trans-Atlantic flight came to Kenley after visiting nearby Croydon Airport.

Empire Air Days began in 1934 and were very popular. The romance of flying and the aerobatic displays drew huge crowds. Douglas Bader was on a flight from Kenley to Woodley aerodrome when he crashed and lost his legs. Undaunted, Bader went on to become one of the most famous RAF pilots of World War II and a national hero.

For almost two years, from 1931, flying stopped at Kenley while rebuilding was carried out. The aerodrome became a storage section and was not reopened until May 1934. Germany's rearmament and increasing military strength led in 1936 to the creation of Fighter Command under Air Marshall Hugh Dowding and the formation of new squadrons. The threat of war caused the RAF Voluntary Reserve to be brought into being and more girls were recruited into the WAAF.

In 1939, two new runways were built which would enable the new Hurricanes and Spitfires to operate more effectively. A 50-foot perimeter track was also laid. When war came, Kenley's crucial position ensured that it would be important in the defence of London and the south of England. It became the headquarters of B Sector, 11 Group, which covered the area to the south from Shoreham to Bexhill on the coast.

While Kenley may not be as well-known as Biggin Hill, it too played a decisive role in the Battle of Britain. From

July to October 1940, Hawker Hurricanes and Spitfires (at least six squadrons of which were based at Kenley) fought Messerschmitts, Heinkels and Dorniers above the Kent and Surrey countryside. From Kenley, 32 airmen and 80 aircraft were lost, many of the crews coming from the Commonwealth, Belgium and Poland. A high price to pay in men and machines.

The high price continued. By the summer of 1941 there were three Spitfire squadrons at Kenley: No.452 Squadron (Royal Australian Air Force); No.485 Squadron (Royal New Zealand Air Force); and No.602 Squadron (The City of Glasgow). As in all wars, the conflict had its share of heroes, many of whom were allied airmen from Australia and New Zealand. Squadron Leader 'Al' Deere had command of No.602 from July 1941 to April 1942. He was a 'Kiwi' of outstanding ability who had been decorated with the Distinguished Flying Cross by King George VI in 1940. A brave, exceptional pilot who sometimes led the Kenley Wing, when he left to become a wing commander at Biggin Hill, he passed command of 602 Squadron to another inspirational flyer, Paddy Finucane who, along with the Australian flight commander, Keith 'Bluey' Truscott, had an impressive rate of success in shooting down German fighters. They became national heroes. Finucane said of his Australian co-pilots, 'I've never met a more loyal and gamer crowd of chaps.'

Truscott was made commander of No.452 Squadron but was called back to Australia because of the Japanese threat. Unfortunately, 'Bluey,' one of his country's most successful Second World War pilots, was killed in his

Kittihawk in an accident off the coast of Western Australia. In Canberra, at the Australian War Memorial, is a Spitfire MKV which was flown by 'Bluey' and his colleagues of No.452 Squadron.

Pilot Officer Johnny Checketts, a 'Kiwi', gained heroic status when, on his second tour of duty, he shot down 13 enemy aircraft. He eventually became commander of No.485 Squadron (RNZAF). He gained the DSO for an action in which he destroyed five Messerschmitt 109's. Having been shot down over France, he was rescued by a French lobster boat and brought back by night to England.

All the heroism was not lost on those in power and there were important visitors to RAF Kenley. The Prime Minister, Winston Churchill, came, as did the Australian politician, Robert Menzies. King George VI spent time watching an operation of the Wing from their flight out, its progress in the operations room and their return. He met the pilots of No.485 and No.602 squadrons, a gesture greatly appreciated by the men.

As the war progressed, the Germans were driven back and squadrons were moved to France. From 1942, the Canadians joined RAF Kenley, an invasion, some said 'not seen since the Roman occupation'. But the need for Kenley lessened. The concrete runways were dangerously short for the larger, more powerful aircraft that were increasingly being used. When control of the sector passed to Biggin Hill in 1945, it was the beginning of the end for Kenley. Flying ceased and the base became a Disarmament School. From 1949-1957 Tiger Moths and Austers were flown from there by the Royal Auxiliary Air Force.

The aerodrome finally closed in 1974. However, the Air Cadet Training Corps use it for gliding at weekends and the Surrey Hills Gliding Club on weekdays. Vestiges of the old aerodrome are still there, the hard runways and perimeter track, but slowly the grass and chalk-downland flowers are taking it back. Where once were Spitfires are now skylarks and instead of Hurricane engines you can hear woodpeckers drumming. In 1983 fifty-two acres were returned to public use. That we are free to walk there is also a fitting tribute to those who fought for that freedom. All honour to their memory.

A VERY RASCALLY PIECE OF EARTH

A VERY RASCALLY PIECE OF EARTH

Progress is a myth. Just look at the M25, the 117 mile London Orbital motorway. First suggested in the early twentieth century, it was finally completed in 1986 and soon afterwards the traffic levels exceeded the maximum designed capacity to carry 88,000 vehicles per day and by 1993 it was carrying 200,000. The stretch between Junctions 13 and 14, near Heathrow Airport, at times exceeds 196,000 vehicles per day. Madness! It is one of the busiest and most congested parts of the British road system. Any fool could have told the planners that the traffic would expand to fill the space available… and then some! No wonder that Terry Pratchett and Neil Gaiman in their comedy-fantasy novel '*Good Omen*' say that the M25 is 'evidence for the hidden hand of Satan in the affairs of Man'. Too true. Who wants to sit in a jam of steaming steel? And, of course, there are other casualties of this symbol of Man's ingenuity.

If walking eastwards along the Millennium Trail, you come down off the south-facing escarpment of Colley and Reigate Hill (owned by the National Trust and part of the Surrey Hills Area of Outstanding Natural Beauty) where, in spring, you will find cowslips, woodanemones, violets, daisies and bluebells, you will leave behind the constant noise of the M25 and, through Great Buck Wood, you will enter Lower Gatton, part of the Manor of Gatton which is bisected by the motorway. The landscape then becomes 'Capability' Brown parkland with sweeping vistas, lakes and great old trees such as cedars of Lebanon, wellingtonias and a chestnut avenue.

Despite the 'improvements' of the 18th century gardener, this is an old landscape and what is now the North Downs Way was once the Pilgrims' Way from the west to Canterbury. Roman artefacts have been found here and the Saxons named it 'Gatton' meaning 'an enclosure besides the way'. The village was destroyed by Danish invaders and by 1066 the manor belonged to King Harold's brother, Leofwin. But not for long, because after the Battle of Hastings, it fell into the hands of Odo, Bishop of Bayeux, half-brother to the victorious William of Normandy. In the great 'housekeeping' inventory, the Domesday Book of 1086, where it appears as 'Gatone', the manor was valued at £6 and, its assets were two hides, six acres of meadow, woodland and herbage worth seven hogs and, it was baldly stated, 'there is a church'.

Since then the manor and the church have had a chequered history, being owned by many people, including King Henry VIII's fourth wife, Anne of Cleves, and, in 1751, Sir James Colebrooke, a banker who hired 'Capability' Brown to improve his park. Gatton also gained some notoriety as a 'rotten' or 'pocket' borough and was called by William Cobbett (1763-1835), the radical reformer, 'a rascally piece of earth'. Such a borough was one where a parliamentary constituency had declined in size but still had the right to elect members to the House of Commons. Many such boroughs were under the control or 'in the pocket' of one man, the patron, and had very few voters. There was no secret ballot and candidates could therefore buy their way to victory and gain undue and unrepresentative influence in Parliament. Just before the Reform Act of 1832, more than 140 parliamentary seats out of a total of 658 were rotten boroughs. Gatton had seven qualified voters in 1831 and 'elected' two MP's. The 'Town Hall', a Doric Temple with an open portico and a roof, was built in 1765. Here 'elections' took place and the 'results' were announced even though they were a foregone conclusion. In 1832 the borough was disenfranchised. Behind the 'Town Hall' is a large urn, erected 'in memory of the deceased borough' which for hundreds of years had been amongst the most rotten in England. Sir Nicholas Pevsner, the architectural historian, said that the small pseudo-classical building was 'one of the best architectural and political jokes in England'.

Ownership of the estate passed through many hands until in 1830 the fifth Lord Monson bought it and set about restoring and refurbishing it. At a time when it was fashionable for the aristocracy to take the Grand Tour, Monson scoured Europe for treasures with which to adorn Gatton Hall and its church. Marbles, paintings, statuary and furnishings for the church poured in. It is the Church of St Andrew at Gatton which draws many visitors today.

Although there are Norman foundations, it is claimed a Saxon church stood here. The present church has a

The Town Hall at Gatton Park, described by Sir Nicholas Pevsner as 'one of the best architectural and political jokes in England'.

hotchpotch appearance, a result of Lord Monson's renovation but it is the interior which is amazing.

The carved stalls are arranged in collegiate style, facing each other, and are of Flemish baroque design with cherubs at each end: no two cherubs have the same expression. Each seat is hinged so that when tipped up, the ledge could be used to relieve monks when they had to stand for hours as they sang the divine offices. Beneath each ledge is a corbel on which the woodcarvers could exercise their art with some freedom because it was more concealed. There are mythical beasts, religious scenes and folk tales. At Gatton there is a variety of faces, some gloomy, some impishly smiling and some showing the Green Man, a popular vegetative myth. Each misericord (from the Latin for 'pity') is carved from a single block of wood. Lord Monson brought these carved stalls from a Benedictine monastery in Ghent.

From Aurschot Cathedral in Louvain he brought the wainscoting and the panelling. The communion rail is from Tongres in Flanders and in the chancel is carved panelling from Burgundy. All these are supreme examples of the woodworkers' art but, perhaps, the masterpieces are the carved panels on the altar and those on the pulpit which show the Descent from the Cross. It is claimed that these came from a reredos designed by Albrecht Durer. What treasures!

On the north side of the nave is the family pew, a small room really, access to which for the Lords of the Manor is by a covered passage from the Hall to the church. Even here in this private pew, the richly-carved woodwork continues on the chairs, benches and in the elaborate surround to the fireplace.

At the west end is a twelfth century open carved work English screen which was rescued when a country church was having a fit of modernisation and it was to be destroyed. See what I mean about progress. How could they? Perhaps we ought to give thanks that Lord Monson saved all these treasures for us to enjoy for it is the woodwork that St Andrew's church is renowned. It is wellworth a visit.

In 1888, Gatton Park was bought by Jeremiah Coleman (of mustard fame) and he too did much to beautify the Hall and grounds. In 1934 the Hall burned down and was later rebuilt. In the Second World War it was used by the army, and in 1948 The Royal Alexandra and Albert Foundation bought it to use as a boarding school. Despite the vicissitudes of the estate, St Andrew's remains a village church even though there is no village and its congregation is far-flung. Get away from the noise and hurry of the M25 and explore Gatton and its church. It'll do you good.

AMBER

AMBER

In 1993, the big movie of the year was '*Jurassic Park*', Steven Spielberg's film version of Michael Crichton's bestselling book in which dinosaurs are genetically recreated from blood taken from ancient mosquitoes found in amber. Not only did this contribute to 'dinomania' amongst children but it stimulated interest in amber which has been called 'a natural time capsule' because it can give us a glimpse of Earth's distant past. I came into closer contact with it while exploring the North Sea coast at the mouth of River Blyth within the Suffolk Coast and Heath Area of Outstanding Natural Beauty.

Amber is a fossil resin from ancient coniferous trees that flourished millions of years ago. The resin is produced by the trees as a protection against insects and, because it has antiseptic properties, against wounds and illnesses. It is viscous, trapping anything that lands on it, whether plant or animal. When the resin hardens it is eventually absorbed into sediment where it changes to form amber. Today there are few tress that have resin that is suitable to become amber, the Kauri pine of New Zealand being one. Unlike diamonds and rubies etc., amber is not a gemstone but an organic gem such as pearls and coral.

This warm, attractive, organic material has long been admired and held in esteem. Because it is easy to carve it has been in use in jewellery since the Stone Age. In one of the Cheddar caves, amber from 10,000 BC was found and a beautiful Bronze Age amber cup was discovered in a tumulus at Hove in Sussex.

The Greeks called it 'elektron', from which 'electricity' is derived: if rubbed it becomes warm and can attract paper. It has been found in Celtic graves and the ancient Irish made beautiful torques of amber and gold. In Rome it was cheaper to buy a slave than amber and Roman matrons regarded it not only as a suitable decoration but as a protection against spells. Maidens wore it to protect their chastity. Anglo-Saxons carried amber amulets for good luck, especially in battle.

Medieval physicians used it as a nostrum, crushed with honey, against the plague and for more common afflictions such as asthma. Its power for good and the ability to ward off the evil eye caused it to be used in religious artefacts such as the amber beads found in rosaries. Many reliquaries were made of precious materials such as gold or silver and amber. Gloriana herself, Queen Elizabeth I, had an amber pomander, carved for her by the court goldsmith.

There must have been quite an extensive trade in amber for even in landlocked Tibet it was used, turquoise being exchanged for it. In the Bronze Age, amber, mainly found on the east coast was exported from Britain. In the past, sailors burned it on their vessels to protect themselves from Leviathan and other monsters from the deep. It is still used in foreign temples to appease gods.

The Amber Tree in The Amber Museum, Southwold, Suffolk. Well worth a visit.

Perhaps the most spectacular use for it was the Amber Room. In 1710, King Fredrick I of Prussia had a room made of amber panels which he later gave to his fellow autocrat, Czar Peter the Great of Russia who installed it in the Winter Palace at St Petersburg. It was moved again to the Ekaterinburg Palace in Tsarkoe Selo. In the Second World War it was looted by the Germans and taken back to Prussia to the Konigsburg Palace. At the end of the war it vanished. Was it destroyed? Is it a hidden treasure in some private collection? No one knows. A panel did come to light in Germany in 1977 but nothing since. However, in 2003, after many years of work by craftsmen and with financial help from Germany, another Amber Room was recreated in the Catherine Palace in St.Petersburg.

Many people think that amber comes only from the Baltic states but it is found in many other places also: Mexico, Burma and the Dominican Republic, to mention a few, all have amber. Even in England we have some, in the Isle of Wight, where many dinosaurs have been discovered, other reminders of our ancient past.

Most of the amber found in the UK is found washed up mainly on the beaches of the east coast counties of Norfolk and Suffolk. In the delightful seaside town of Southwold, in the market place, is The Amber Shop which deals in this unique gem. Not only are the goods on show alluring but one can also visit the Amber Museum, dedicated to telling the story of this fascinating gem. It is well worth a visit.

Much of the amber in Britain has been brought over the millennia by ocean currents and savage storms from countries around the Baltic Sea. There are huge deposits in the Samland peninsula, part of that strangely detached bit of Russia, Kaliningrad, which lies between Poland and Lithuania.

The most common and favoured colours of amber are yellow, brown or tawny gold but there are other colourstoo. Some Mexican amber is green or blue, Sicilian can be black and Burmese can be red or orange. It can be easily faked,

Southwold, home of the Amber Museum

using such substances as glass, celluloid or plastic. Unscrupulous dealers even go to the extent of drilling holes and inserting insects or plants because amber with inclusions is more valuable. What they forget is that the specimens must be contemporaneous with the amber and not modern. Thus they are easily caught out and their trickery exposed.

However, there are tests for amber. Press a red-hot pin against the surface and the smell should be resinous if it is genuine. Amber will float in sea water and it is possible to scratch amber whereas glass does not scratch easily. Real amber is warm to the touch. In fact, too much heat causes it to dry out and crack.

Next time you're taking a stroll along the East Anglian coast, especially after a storm, take care where you tread and look carefully because you may find amber, a beautiful reminder of a time when dinosaurs walked the earth.

AMETHYST

AMETHYST

'The sea's a long way from here,' I think as I stare at the church notice board which shows a boat, its sail filled out by a stiff wind which also churns up the sea. The church in question is that of St Peter in Tandridge, Surrey, where I'd gone after the urging of a fellow walker who said I might be interested in what was there. He didn't specify, but knowing that, like Shakespeare's Autolycus, I am 'a snapper up of unconsidered trifles', I would have to go to see what he was on about.

'Perhaps it's symbolic,' and I rummage around in my noddle for the answer. St Peter was a fisherman, wasn't he? And didn't Jesus calm the fears of his disciples on a storm-tossed Sea of Galilee like the Church tossed about on the sea of doubt and opposition. Isn't the word 'nave' from the Latin 'navis'(a ship)? And (a bit recondite this) didn't one of the Church Fathers, St Clement of Alexandria, say that 'the vessel flying before the wind' is one of the symbols of the early church? It's obviously the barque of St Peter. Sorted! And I enter the churchyard to begin my exploration.

It's an attractive church with its shingle spire, the whole building being overshadowed by an enormous yew tree (about which I have written in another chapter). As before, the church itself was locked but on the notice board in the porch there was a cutting from 'Navy News' for September 2009, which was entitled 'Veterans recall heroes of the Yangtze Incident' with a photograph of the then minister and assorted naval folk and Union flags decorating the porch. Intrigued, I read the piece and knew that this was what my friend had meant me to see and explore.

In December 1948 during the Chinese civil war, a British warship HMS Consort was stationed at Nanking in order to protect and rescue those at our embassy and others of our nationals who might get caught up in the troubles. In April 1949, HMS Amethyst while en route on the River Yangtze to relieve the Consort, was fired upon and seriously damaged. She went aground on Rose Island and signalled that she was still under fire and had casualties on board, including the Captain, Lt. Commander Skinner who was fatally wounded. Attempts were made to evacuate ashore those who were lightly wounded and some uninjured crew but this was stopped when the Communist troops fired on those in the water.

HMS Consort had heard the signal and went to the assistance of the Amethyst. She too came under heavy fire, so much so that after three failed attempts and much loss of life, she abandoned the rescue. But, fortunately, HMS Black Swan and HMS London had heard the signal too and went to help.

By this time, April 21st, the Amethyst had been re-floated and anchored in the river while the Black Swan and the London got within 30 miles of her and waited for further information but because none was forthcoming,

The church sign at St Peter's, Tandridge, Surrey.

Walking group at the church sign of St Peter's, Tandridge, Surrey. The author is to the immediate left of the sign, holding it for support BEFORE a walk. Speaks volumes, doesn't it?

both vessels hoisted white ensigns and large white flags, signifying neutrality. To no avail, for the Chinese troops continued firing and they received direct hits. They had to retreat and did so under fire.

An RAF Sunderland flying boat landed near the Amethyst with a doctor and medical supplies. The firing kept on and the Sunderland had to take off quickly.

On April 22nd, Lt Cdr J S Kerans arrived to take command of the stricken vessel which was to remain a prisoner in the River Yangtze for a hundred days in total. The new captain realised that something had to be done and he decided to make a run for it under cover of darkness, an audacious plan. He waited until July 30th, when the river would be at its highest and then started downriver under fire. She took one hit but there were no more and the Amethyst continued her escape until she met HMS Concord at the mouth of the river and the famous message was then sent: 'Have rejoined the fleet south of Woosung, no damage or casualties. God Save the King'.

This great escape made naval history and became the stuff of legend. 46 sailors died and many awards were made. A film was made of it in 1957, 'The Yangtze Incident,' which celebrated a remarkable story of courage and discipline, with Richard Todd as the heroic captain.

It was the 60th anniversary of the end of this episode that was being featured in the 'Navy News' for Lieutenant Commander John Kerans, CO of HMS Amethyst is buried in St Peter's churchyard. After the service, which included newsreel footage, there was a procession to his grave where tributes were laid to the 33 year-old naval attaché who took the Amethyst more than 140 miles down a dark river with no charts and under the constant firing from the Communist guns. Great stuff! And when I think about it, how appropriate it now seems that the church-sign should show a ship escaping a storm. St Peter's barque and HMS Amethyst are as one.

AN EARLY ECO-WARRIOR

AN EARLY ECO-WARRIOR

There's nothing new under the sun. In these days of 'sit-ins' at St Paul's cathedral, protest marches against nuclear power and attacks on wind farms which blight the countryside, we might be forgiven for thinking that deforestation, pollution and global warming, general concern for the planet we live on, are new menaces in the forefront of ethical discussion all over the world. However, such discussion is not new.

Those travelling today along the busy A200 road (the old Dover Road) through the multicultural Thames-side London suburb of Deptford may be unaware of its rich and colourful history. From a small fishing village in pre-Tudor times it developed into a bustling maritime town when King Henry VIII established the Royal Naval Dockyard there in 1513. It grew to be the size of Bristol and has now become part of the ever-spreading urban sprawl of the capital.

One of Deptford's most colourful inhabitants was John Evelyn (1620-1706), known mainly today for his diary, which he called his 'Kalendarium' and which covered the years 1646-1706. In it he paints vivid portraits of his contemporaries, such as that other famous diarist, Samuel Pepys, and he gives us some idea of the social and cultural life of the latter half of the seventeenth century. 'Keep a diary and some day it'll keep you,' said the American actress Mae West. Unfortunately for Evelyn, this wasn't the case because his diary wasn't discovered until 1813 in an old clothes basket.

Evelyn's life was long: he lived during the reigns of James I, Charles I, the Interregnum, Charles II, James II, William and Mary and Queen Anne. He witnessed the Civil War, The Restoration of the monarchy, the plague and the Great Fire of London, and much of this is recorded in his minute, almost illegible script. He was a founder member of The Royal Society which counted Wren, Boyle and Newton among its members.

Although most famous for his '*Kalendarium*,' he wrote about thirty books which showed the breadth of his interests, history, religion, the arts and, most influential, horticulture. He was a botanist and tree expert and his book '*Sylva or a Discourse on Forest Trees*,' published by The Royal Society, brought attention to silviculture and matters ecological. He was greatly concerned with the rapid deforestation of the countryside by such causes as iron smelting, the charcoal industry and, especially, the heavy consumption of timber in the ship building industry: the 'wooded walls' which protected our island were bought at a great price to our woodlands.

Evelyn promoted reafforestation, not only as a damage limitation exercise or the restoration of a degraded eco-system but also to provide timber for shipbuilding in the

The grounds at Wotton House, once the Evelyn family home, now a luxury hotel and conference centre.

The Evelyn family mausoleum at Wotton, the family estate.

An Early Eco-Warrior 47

future. Possibly, without his timely warning, Nelson wouldn't have had all the ships he needed in the wars with the French in the late eighteenth and early nineteenth centuries. Where would we have been then, mes amis?

'*Sylva*' had an appendix called '*Pomona: Concerning Fruit Trees*', both being published in 1664 and remaining the standard text book on tree propagation and planting for the next two hundred years and more. In this way, Evelyn had a great influence on the look of our countryside and its great estates.

He was a great traveller, journeying through France, Germany and Italy, returning with a wealth of ideas, especially about gardening. Although the family home was Wotton House in Surrey, Evelyn had Sayes Court in Deptford built for him and here he put into practice some of the ideas he had gleaned while abroad. His garden in the French style became famous and here he retreated during the years of the Commonwealth (1649-60).

Unfortunately, Peter the Great, Czar of Muscovy, in pursuit of his great idea of modernising his court and empire, came to England to study shipbuilding and rented Sayes Court. Peter was a great carouser and would get drunk most evenings and trash the house and gardens. He would get his men to push him a wheelbarrow through the flower beds and parterres and once through a much-prized holly hedge. On his departure, Evelyn recorded in his diary that he went to Deptford 'to view how miserably the Czar of Muscovy had left my house'. Sir Christopher Wren, the King's Surveyor, inspected the damage and Evelyn was awarded £150, a huge sum at that time. All that remains of

Evelyn's estate in south east London are some street names and a sad little patch of a park.

The main estate of the Evelyns, whose fortune was based on a royal monopoly for the making of gunpowder, was near Dorking, Surrey, at Wotton House, and it is here that much of John Evelyn's remaining work as a 'landscape gardener' (not a term known then) can be seen. With the help of his brother, George, who had inherited the estate, he designed the gardens, eschewing the formalism of Tudor gardens which had been in vogue for some time for a more Italian style. In the well-watered valley the house is set, he created an elaborate fountain, temples and, centrally, a multi-level mount.

Not far away, at Albury Park, there are the remains of the garden he created for Henry Howard in 1667: the terraces, a long canal and, somewhat strange this, a tunnel in which two coaches abreast could be driven.

In his 'Almanac' of 1666, the year of the Great Fire of London, Evelyn gave advice to his readers about what to do in their gardens each month with useful tips such as using 'tobacco waste' as a weed killer. There are also illustrations of gardening tools which we would find familiar today.

Although Sayes Court in Deptford had comparatively clean air, London itself, because of the sea coal that was burned, was covered by a 'hellish and dismal cloud' that 'covered everything with thick, black soot'. In another book, *'Fumifugium or the Inconvenience of the Air and Smoke of London Dissipated'* (1662), Evelyn suggested that a green belt should be established around the capital to get rid of the miasma that hung over it. Such a belt, he said, could be planted with sweet-smelling herbs and fragrant shrubs, the clippings from which could be burnt in the city streets to get rid of the pervasive stench. Yes, Evelyn's green concerns make him a forerunner of today's eco-warriors, indeed.

AN UNSUNG HERO OF
MEDICINE

AN UNSUNG HERO OF MEDICINE

Teachers catch everything from their pupils. What goes around, comes around, and daily contact with snivelling, scratching and coughing kids usually meant that I'd get whatever it was next. Had chickenpox thrice. I know, I know, you can't have it more than once everybody says. Well, whatever I had was a damn good imitation of the disease.

One of my favourite walks is in Dorset, from Worth Matravers, a picturesque village of limestone cottages around a duck pond where the main industries are farming, quarrying and fishing, down through Winspit, along the coast past the limestone quarries and caves, back up onto St Aldhelm's Head with its square Norman chapel and then along the fieldway path to the National Trust car park at my starting point and a drink in 'The Square and Compass', a splendid local pub with a small museum exhibiting fossils and local artefacts. It was on such a walk that I explored the village church of St Nicholas of Smyrna (the original Santa Claus) and came across the grave of an unsung hero of medicine.

Smallpox, a contagious, feverish and often fatal disease, characterised by pus-filled eruptions called 'pocks'(and called 'small' to distinguish it from syphilis, 'the great pox') at one time affected 10 to 15 million people globally and two million died annually from it. This devastating pestilence had been known though all ages and in most places. In London, the Smallpox Hospital which had originally stood on the site of King's Cross Station in 1846 was rebuilt and enlarged in north London.

From 1967-75, through a network of fieldworkers, scientists and bacteriological and virological laboratories which conduct research and assist in the diagnosis, prevention and control of communicable diseases, the World Health Organisation campaign to eradicate smallpox was successful. In October 1977 the last naturally occurring case was recorded, and in 1980 the disease was declared extinct. Now, apart from one or two special laboratories, such as the government establishment at Porton Down where a few samples are kept under the strictest security, smallpox, one of the main scourges of mankind for thousands of years, is no more. Its eradication was one of the most important scientific achievements of the twentieth century.

However, some two hundred years earlier in the Dorset village of Yetbury, deep in Hardy country, a local farmer, Benjamin Jesty, had successfully vaccinated his family against smallpox. Country lore held that milkmaids were immune to smallpox because they had at some time contracted cowpox. Traditional reactions to the disease were either to flee the district or apply a poultice of soot and butter; there are no figures to show how efficacious the latter remedy was.

The graves of Benjamin Jesty and his wife in St Nicholas' churchyard, Worth Matravers.

Jesty had observed that two of his milkmaids, who had both had cowpox, came from families that were suffering from the then current outbreak of smallpox yet they themselves had not contracted it. He conceived the idea of giving his wife and children cowpox by artificial means. He took his wife, Elizabeth, and his two boys to a nearby farm where he took a sample from an infected cow and, using a needle, injected the matter into the arms of his family. This vaccination, from the Latin 'vacca' for cow, was recorded for the first time in 1774, twenty-two years before Dr Edward Jenner's first vaccination experiment.

There had been other methods of combating the disease before this and in other countries. Lady Mary Wortley Montagu (1689-1762), wife of the British ambassador in Constantinople, had recorded in her diary for July 17th 1723, that her sister's son had died of smallpox despite Lady Mary's offer of performing on him variolation which she had performed on her own children: this was the method whereby the dried crust of a smallpox lesion was applied to the nasal mucous membrane. It was a method known and used in the Middle and Far East for hundreds of years.

The far more well-known scientist Edward Jenner, son of a country vicar, had proved the connection between cowpox and smallpox, but he first did it in 1796 and not from cow to human but from human to human, taking a sample from a dairymaid and injecting it into the arm of a young boy. While there were many people, learned doctors as well as the ignorant and often superstitious country folk who opposed vaccination, its popularity grew as its success became apparent. In 1800, by command of the Duke of York, the army was vaccinated and in 1801 so was the Mediterranean fleet.

Jenner, as we know, went on to become rich and famous. He was voted £30,000 by Parliament, an immense sum for those days. The King of Prussia rewarded him, the French Emperor, Napoleon III, sent him 500 francs, and eventually a statue of the Gloucestershire doctor was proposed for Trafalgar Square, though it ended up in Kensington Gardens. Despite efforts by well-meaning friends to bring Jesty's

Worth Matravers, Dorset, where Benjamin Jesty is buried.

accomplishment to the public notice, the Dorset farmer didn't achieve fame and riches. He visited London to address the Vaccine Pock Institution where he demonstrated publicly his faith in his method by being vaccinated himself, as was his son who accompanied him. He returned to his new home in Worth Matravers with an illuminated testimonial and a pair of gold-mounted lancets.

He died in 1816 and is buried in the church of St Nicholas at Worth. On his headstone his wife Elizabeth had inscribed:

Sacred
To the Memory
Of
Benj.Jesty
Who departed this life
April 16th 1816
Aged 79 years
… an upright honest
Man particularly noted for
Having been the first person (known)
That introduced Cow-Pox
By inoculation…… ..
……… In the year 1774

In this attractive dry-stone village, near the Dorset Coastal Path, beneath ancient yew trees, lies Benjamin Jesty, an unsung hero of medicine.

AUR CYMRU: WELSH GOLD

AUR CYMRU: WELSH GOLD

On Friday 29th April, 2011, Catherine Middleton married Prince William, eldest son of HRH Prince Charles, heir to the British throne. At the age of 29, she was the oldest spinster to marry a future king. There have been two older women who married kings-in-waiting: Camilla, Duchess of Cornwall was 57 when she became Charles' second wife and Eleanor of Aquitaine was 30 when she took as her second husband, Henry II. Both these women were divorcees. Apart from taking on a job which would daunt most women, Catherine had other things in common with British female royals, especially the most recent ones.

Most people associate Welsh mining with the coalmines of the South Wales valleys such as the Rhondda or the slate quarries of North Wales. But gold, too, has been mined. Because of its purity, rarity and difficulty of extraction, Welsh gold (Aur Cymru) has long been a most sought after metal, more expensive than platinum. Gold with the Red Dragon of Wales stamp on it has a high market value.

Although pre-Roman mining of gold may have been limited, the Celts mined it and while no traces remain of their small, near-the-surface mines, their artistic legacy can be seen in beautifully crafted brooches, torques and other jewellery. The work of Celtic goldsmiths was known abroad. Strabo, the Greek historian and geographer, wrote that gold was one of the chief exports of these islands, along with silver and hunting dogs.

In AD 43, the Emperor Claudius invaded Britain and by AD 78 Wales had become part of the Roman Empire. There was expansion of mining for lead, copper, iron and, in the remote hills of south-west Wales, the Romans had an important goldmine at Dolaucothi in Cardiganshire, near the village of Pumpsaint on the A482 road between Lampeter and Llandeilo. Here they had a complex, technically-advanced system of panning for gold with miles of aqueducts and reservoirs. They worked partly by opencast and partly by driving their chisels into the veins. Mineral rights were an Imperial monopoly and at Segontium near Caernarfon there was a procurator in charge of Imperial mining. Now the National Trust owns the land, and the industrial remains, including the bathhouse, are exhibited. In the summer months it is possible to visit the workings, and visitors wearing helmets and stout footwear can pan for gold and take guided tours.

In North Wales, beneath Cader Idris where three of their roads meet, the Romans mined gold near the market town of Dolgellau (which may mean 'Meadow of Hazels' or 'Meadow of Slaves', forced labour perhaps) between AD 75-140.

In the sixteenth century, by the two Acts of Union, the mining rights became the property of the Crown; The Company of Mines Royal leased their rights to

Dolauciothi Gold Mine, Carmarthenshire, where visitors to this National Trust site can tour Roman and more modern underground workings and pan for gold.

Aur Cymru: Welsh Gold 63

contractors. At one stage the mining was financed by German capital and German workers mined for gold. In the early seventeenth century, a goldsmith Hugh Myddleton, took over the rights. From 1700 onwards mining rights were granted by licence from the owner of the soil. Royalties are still paid to the Crown on any gold mined in Wales.

However, it was not until Victorian times when more finds were made, making mining financially viable, that the industry became re-established. Dolgellau, the small grey town where Owain Glyndwr had assembled the last Welsh Parliament in 1404, became a booming Welsh Klondike as prospectors panned the streams and rivers and hundreds of miners were employed in more than 20 mines. It is claimed that almost three-quarters of the total British gold produced at this time came from one mine alone, the Clogau St David's mine.

It wasn't only Celtic chieftains who had a taste for Welsh gold. Later Welsh kings and princes adorned themselves with elaborate gold jewellery. The connection with royalty continues, for when Princess May of Teck, later to become Queen Mary, married the prince who was to become King George V in 1893, their wedding rings were made of this rare and precious metal. Our present Queen has a wedding ring made from a nugget of 22 carat Welsh gold which was presented to her father, the then Duke of York in 1923, to make a wedding ring for his fiancée, Lady Elizabeth Bowes Lyon. Such was the size of the nugget, from the Clogau St David's mine in Bontddu, Gwynedd, that Princes Margaret's wedding ring was made from it in 1960, Princess Anne's in 1973 and the Princess of Wales' in 1981. At the Investiture of the Prince of Wales at Caernarfon Castle in 1963, the regalia was made of gold from nearby mines.

In 1981, the Royal British Legion presented to Her Majesty Queen Elizabeth II, a new 36 grammes bar of 22 carat Clogau gold From this was made Sarah Ferguson's ring when she married Prince Andrew in 1986 and, when Prince Edward married Sophie Rhys-Jones, now Countess of Wessex, their wedding rings were made from Welsh gold. And on April 29th 2011, HRH Prince William, Duke of Cambridge, slipped a ring of Welsh gold onto the finger of his new wife, Catherine, Duchess of Cambridge. The tradition continues.

Welsh gold is rare because, unlike much gold which is concentrated in veins, it is found scattered in auriferous quartz, and to produce even a small amount many tons of rock have to be moved. It has long been held that this gold has a warmer, reddish hue, almost pink. Much Victorian gold jewellery was of this colour. In order to protect reserves, it was mixed with silver or copper, thus giving it a rose colour. However, Welsh gold, in reality, is the same colour yellow as any other. Archaeologists can use sophisticated analysing devices to trace the origins of any gold jewellery they find, thus ensuring the provenance of any with claims to be Welsh. The technique is also used by detectives in pursuit of gold thieves.

Although by the second half of the nineteenth century more than £5 million pounds of gold (by today's value) had been mined, because of such problems as transport and distance, gold mining has never really been a successful venture. The Welsh gold rush did not last long and the mines began to close in the 1920s. One of the last was Gwynfynydd (White Mountain) mine which, although it had a disastrous fire in 1935, continued up to April 1988. Output was controlled and only three goldsmiths were licensed to use it. A geological survey of the Clogau mine has claimed that mining might be viable. Some extraction from the waste tips has been carried out.

However, the lure of Welsh gold has given impetus to the Welsh tourist industry, for visitors can follow a Gold Trail from Dolaucothi with its Roman remains and National Trust activities, via the Welsh Gold Centre in the small mid-Wales rural town of Tregaron, to the North Wales goldfield. You never know, there might still be 'gold in them there hills' for some.

CENOTAPHS

CENOTAPHS

Strange word, 'cenotaph'. It comes from the Greek for 'empty tomb'. It is the name given to the block of Portland stone in the middle of the road in Whitehall which has become the centrepiece of our national ritual of mourning on Armistice Day November 11th and Remembrance Sunday two days later.

It has a number of unusual features. There is not a straight line in its construction. The Greeks had discovered the principle of 'entasis': that if a column is built with vertical lines, it will look as though it narrows in the middle. To counteract this, an outward curve makes it look straight. Another feature which is often overlooked by many is that there is no religious symbolism in its construction. It is a memorial to the dead of many nations, each with their own belief system and therefore there is no specific reference to any particular religion such as Christianity.

Everyone refers to the structure as the Cenotaph and this too is a mistake for the 'empty tomb' is the flat altar-slab on the top: the rest is simply the obelisk that supports it. That it is where it is makes an interesting story.

When the Great War (1914-1918) was over, it was decided to have a victory parade through the capital to give thanks for its end and to honour those who had given their lives. Represenatives from all the nationalities who had fought with us, French, Belgian, American, and all our allies from the Empire, were to march along the grand processional route. It was felt that some kind of monument was needed to act as a focus, and Prime Minister Lloyd George thought this a good idea.

Edwin Lutyens, the architect of New Delhi was given the job but had little time to design anything permanent, so a temporary structure of wood, canvas and plaster was put up. It proved such a success with the parading troops who all saluted it, as did many of the crowd, that Lloyd George and the government announced that it was to be built in a permanent form. By December 1920 it had been rebuilt in stone at the same time that the tomb of the Unknown Soldier was established in Westminster Abbey. At this memorial to 'The Glorious Dead' a service is held annually at which the monarch and leading politicians lay tribute to those who made the supreme sacrifice. It is followed at exactly eleven o'clock by two minutes silence after which there is a procession of thousands of ex-service personnel with accompanying recognition and applause from the thousands who line the route, especially for the maimed and injured. The eleventh hour of the eleventh day of the eleventh month is a sacred moment for the nation.

And now let us move to a more modest but nonetheless poignant cenotaph and ceremony.

In Roman times, the Wealden forest of Anderida stretched for over a hundred miles across south-east England. Today only tracts of it remain, of which the

The Cenotaph in Whitehall

Ashdown Forest is the largest, part of that quarter of Sussex which is woodland. In common ownership and private, this stretch of moorland, heath and woods is the largest public access area in the south and is designated not only an Area of Outstanding Natural Beauty but also as a Site of Special Scientific Interest and a European Special Protection Area.

A board of conservators manages the forest and ten full-time staff carry out the day-to-day tasks involved in looking after the huge area, 6,500 acres, which attracts thousands of visitors not only for the natural beauty found along its network of footpaths and bridleways, but also for its literary and historical associations.

The author, A A Milne lived on a farm near Hartfield, and the forest is the background for the adventures of his most famous creation, Winnie the Pooh. There are two stretches of Roman road, the remains of the 28 km 'pale', the ditch and bank which once enclosed the forest when it was a royal hunting ground. Pillow mounds can be found where rabbits, introduced by the Normans in the twelfth century, were bred for their fur and meat. You can also find the remains of the old airstrip built as an exercise by Canadian engineers in the Second World War. But perhaps the most visited site is the Airman's Grave, found in the grazed southern portion of the forest.

Victor Sutton was eighteen when he joined the RAF in March 1935. His father had fought in the Great War, 1914-1918, where he had been wounded. He died in 1922 as part of the British Occupation Army of the Rhineland, leaving his wife Elsie to bring up four children, one of whom, Cyril, the eldest, was killed in a traffic accident.

The early stages of the war saw an expansion of the forces and Victor Sutton applied to the RAF and was accepted for training as a pilot. He joined 142 Squadron which was stationed at RAF Binbrook in north Lincolnshire and was equipped with Wellington twin-engine bombers. Victor was assigned to W5364.

Nearly half a million people were in the British Bomber Command and the American 8th Air Force during World War II: of the 125,000 from the RAF, 55,573 died, 8,403 were wounded and 9,838 were captured. In his excellent

The Airman's Grave in the Ashdown Forest. Here Sgt. PVR Sutton, aged 24 years, 142 SQDN RAF, with his five comrades, lies. They lost their lives through enemy action on July 31st 1941 while returning from a raid on Cologne.

history 'Bomber Boys: Fighting Back 1940-45', Patrick Bishop says that for a bomber crew 'life expectancy was considerably shorter than that of a junior infantry officer in 1916'. All Bomber Command aircrew were volunteers and the RAF never wanted for recruits.

Victor's squadron, 142, was declared operational in April 1941, by which time he had married. Much of the flying was done by night so the conditions can be imagined, cramped and cold in the darkness in a plane carrying explosives, full of fuel with enemy fighters and ground installations firing at you as you searched for your targets, military depots, electricity stations, factories, oil refineries, all of which were essential to the German war machine.

Towards the end of July 1941, bad weather curtailed flying operations, but on July 30th they were resumed. Victor's 142 Squadron was sent to attack Cologne's transport system even though the weather was still not ideal. By this time, Victor, now a Sergeant, had become Second Pilot. All together, 116 aircraft were sent, of which six were Wellingtons; four returned. Victor's was one which did not, partly, it is thought, because of the bad weather causing poor visibility and partly because the port engine was damaged.

W5364 went down in the Ashdown Forest, its faltering descent heard in scattered villages such as Nutley and Fairways. Victor had been only seven weeks on the squadron. His mother, Elsie, a London resident, who had already lost her husband was so heartbroken that she moved to Nutley, the village nearest the crash, and put up a small white wooden cross on the place where Victor and his comrades had died, and the clearing was surrounded by a wire fence. In 1954, the wooden cross was replaced by a stone one and a plaque was added to the sandstone wall which was put up in place of the fence. All the names, ranks and ages of the crew were inscribed; the oldest was 27. Victor was 24.

It's strange how local customs originate and develop but since the late 1970s Remembrance Day services have been held at the site, beautifully kept, and it is a place of quiet contemplation . Elsie died, age 90, before these began so she didn't get to see the horseriders, walkers and many others who gather, often in poor weather, to remember and honour her son and his mates.

The place is called 'The Airman's Grave' and, like Lutyens' far grander memorial to the nation's dead in Whitehall, it is a cenotaph, an empty grave, for Victor is buried with his brother, Cyril and mother, Elsie, in plot Y676 at Brockley Cemetery in south-east London. Ironically, his father is buried in Cologne, from whence Victor was returning on the night of the fatal crash in the Ashdown Forest.

EDITH

EDITH

What is it about trains and young boys? 'Where's the train?' Toby asked for the nth time. As did the scores of other kids who were accompanying grannies and granddads to '*The Railway Children*', Edith Nesbit's ever popular story of a prosperous Edwardian family who are forced to move house and live in reduced circumstances when the father is falsely imprisoned on suspicion of being a spy. All the 'oldies' presumably remembered the book and film from their youth but this time around, it was something special. It was being presented as a play and was being staged in the disused Eurostar terminal and platforms at Waterloo Station with a real, live steamtrain, a 140-year-old Stirling Single, as the star of the show. It was a huge success.

When Noel Coward, actor, playwright and wit, died in 1973, on his bedside table lay a copy of Edith Nesbit's '*The Enchanted Castle*'. The Master knew her and was an admirer of her work, especially her children's stories which he reread each year, finding her writing 'light and unforced' and her ability to tell a story 'riveting'.

Edith Nesbit (1858-1924) is best remembered as a writer of children's books, but long before they became successful she had been writing short stories, romantic novels and poetry (influenced by her meeting the Rossettis and their circle of friends). She made her first appearance in print with a poem 'The Dream' published in '*The Saturday Magazine*' when she was eighteen.

She was born in Kennington when it was still semi-rural, where her father, John Nesbit, had a small farm: the area had yet to become a busy, built-up London suburb. He died when Edith was four years old and her mother took her to live in France where she was educated at a convent. They returned to England in 1872 and settled in Halstead, then in the Kent countryside, now a part of the London Borough of Bromley. This south-east part of the capital was where Edith was to have a number of homes, living at various times in Lewisham and Eltham as well as at Halstead.

She married young, at 22, Hubert Bland, a journalist, two months before the birth of her son, Paul. The marriage was unorthodox, almost an open one. Bland, a compulsive womaniser, had many affairs, one of which was with Alice Hoatson, a close friend of Edith, who was acting as their housekeeper and who had two children by Hubert which Edith brought up as her own.

Edith had affairs with other men, mostly younger than herself. As a lifelong committed socialist and, with her husband, a founder of the Fabian Society for the spread of socialist attitudes (Hubert was the first Secretary), she became friendly with Beatrice and Sidney Webb, R H Tawney, H G Wells and G B Shaw with whom Edith had an 'intense but unconsummated friendship'. In fact, Shaw called her 'an audaciously unconventional lady' and Hubert 'an unfaithful husband'. Perhaps ideas about free love and

St Mary in the Marsh – note the wooden grave marker of the author Edith Nesbit – it is a barge-board carved by her husband.

Utopia were in the air. Shaw said of the couple, 'No two people ever married who were better calculated to make the worst of each other.'

After the wedding, their finances needed bolstering so Edith continued writing articles, stories and poems, rather like the mother in *'The Railway Children'*, but it was not until the publication and success of *'The Treasure Seekers'* in 1899 that she found not only her true vocation but financial success at the age of 41.

As with many other authors whose lives inform their work, Edith Nesbit was no different. Not only did people

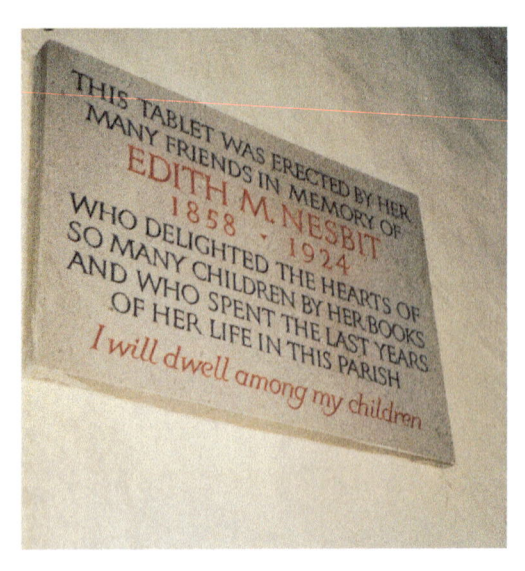

St Mary in the Marsh in Romney Marsh, in the churchyard of which Edith Nesbit is buried.

from her life become characters in her books but places and incidents did so too. In no story is this more apparent than 'The Enchanted Castle', one of Coward's favourites, when the children discover 'Yalding Towers' where the estate bears more than a passing resemblance to the grounds of the Crystal Palace at Sydenham with its prehistoric monsters, into one of which, the dinosaur, Edith's brother had given her a leg-up through a hole in its stomach. She had lived close by and used the location in her book when Mabel helped Kathleen to climb into one of the monsters.

Besides this success, there were others: '*The Would-be Goods*' (1901), '*Five Children and It*'(1902), '*The New Treasure Seekers*'(1904) and the most famous of all, '*The Railway

Children' (1907). While there are critics who find it sentimental, it has remained a perennial favourite and has been made into a number of films and a TV series.

Her best-loved novel, episodic in structure because it first appeared in *'The London Magazine'* in serial form, tells the story of three children whose circumstances become reduced and the family is forced to move to a country cottage when the father disappears from the scene. Peter, Phyllis and Roberta (Bobbie) have adventures, centred mainly on the railway which runs nearby and, eventually, and inevitably, all turns out well and father is cleared of the charge against him. All ends happily.

While there might be an element of wistfulness in it, as in other of her works, perhaps the reason for the success of her children's books lies not simply in a good story, well-told, but that her boys and girls are recognisable, they are real. Edith Nesbit has been called the 'first modern writer for children' because of this.

Her work was publically recognised not simply by its financial success but by the award of a Civil List pension of £60 p.a. in 1915. In 1917, after her first husband died, she married a marine engineer, Thomas Tucker, known as 'The Skipper' who was devoted to her, and they moved to Romney Marsh. They settled in the village of St Mary's in the Marsh where she died in 1924. She was buried under an elm in the churchyard, as she requested, with a wooden marker made by 'The Skipper'. In the church is a plaque which tells how 'she delighted the hearts of so many children'. Who could ask more than that?

Fitter for an History than a Sermon

FITTER FOR AN HISTORY THAN A SERMON

We were staying in Carlisle (home of the Eddie Stobart group for those of you into trucks and trailers) and decided to go on that wonderfully scenic Settle to Carlisle railway. This we did and, en route, thought we'd break our journey at Appleby-in-Westmoreland, famous for its Horse Fair, established in 1685, held at the beginning of June each year and which attracts a huge gypsy gathering from all over Europe.

Situated in a bend of the River Eden, Appleby is an attractive market town with an uncommonly wide main street, Boroughgate, which is one of the finest in England. It also has many handsome buildings attesting to its long and obviously prosperous history. In one of these, St Lawrence's church, we came across the tomb of Lady Anne Clifford whose name I'd seen elsewhere in the small town, on the Almshouses. 'Who's this lady? The name Clifford rings a bell,' I thought, and on investigation I discovered a fascinating story.

We have more than our fair share of feisty women in British history: Boudicca, who gave the Romans a run for their money; the Empress Matilda who would-be Queen of

England but failed to reach the throne, Eleanor of Aquitaine, her daughter-in-law and ambitious wife of Henry II; Elizabeth I, the last and most glorious of the Tudor monarchs, to mention a few (and I can think of an ex-headmistress who could have felled King Kong). To this distinguished list can be added Lady Anne Clifford (1590-1676). She lived through the reigns of four monarchs: Elizabeth I, James I, Charles I, the Interregnum and Charles II, and, at a time when women were their husbands' chattels, she remained resolutely herself even though she married two powerful and influential aristocrats.

Anne Clifford was born at Skipton Castle in Westmorland on June 30th 1590 and was the only surviving child of George Clifford, 3rd Earl of Cumberland, and Margaret Russell, daughter of the Earl of Bedford. Clifford had been appointed Queen's Champion, carrying the monarch's favour in the lists at tournaments. His daughter, 'much beloved by the renowned Queen Elizabeth', was brought up at court as well as at her father's extensive estates.

The Elizabethan poet and scholar, Samuel Daniel, was her tutor and found her a willing pupil, eager to learn the classics, history and poetry which he taught her. She took part in court masques written by Ben Jonson and wore costumes designed for her by Inigo Jones. As a beauty and an heiress, Lady Anne would make a fine match for one of the many eligible nobles at court.

In 1603 the old Queen died, and with the passing of Gloriana a new era of change began, not only for the country but for Lady Anne herself. In 1605 her father died

Lady Anne's tomb at St Lawrence's church, Appleby.

The Clifford tomb in St Lawrence's church, Appleby.

and, to the surprise of all, having made some provision for his widow, the now Dowager Countess Margaret, and his only child and putative heir, Anne, he had left his vast estates in Cumberland, Yorkshire and Westmorland to his brother and his brother's son.

It was then that the old grey matter got into gear and I remembered the fair Rosamond Clifford, mistress of King Henry II who, it is alleged, was poisoned by his jealous wife, Eleanor of Aquitaine. The name Clifford was the first in the acronym 'Cabal' which stood for that group of King Charles II's ministers, Clifford, Arlington, Buckingham, Ashley and Lauderdale, who united to promote their own interests. Must be the same family, surely? I also recalled from the recesses that somewhere in 'King Henry VI Part III', Shakespeare calls Clifford 'proud northern lord' but the adjectives could be equally applied to Lady Anne, for when her patrimony was given into other hands, Clifford blood made her a 'proud northern lady' who for the next almost forty years fought to regain it.

In February 1609, at the age of 19, Lady Anne married Richard Sackville, also 19, who became Earl of Dorset. As his countess, she became mistress of Knole in Kent, one of the great houses of England. She had five children, of whom two daughters survived. However much being a wife and mother may have occupied her, she continued to state her claim to her inheritance. Her husband, something of a 'playboy', was a favourite at the court of King James I and while he hoped to benefit in some way from his wife's claim, he did little to support it.

When the King himself intervened to settle the

conflicting claims, Lady Anne, while recognising the intentions of the monarch, refused to deny her claims to Westmorland while she lived. Nothing availed King James and she stuck to her guns even though the eventual judgment was to go against her.

Another blow was the death of her dear mother, the Dowager Countess Margaret who always supported her and fought for the recognition of her claim. Now Anne felt even more bereft.

There was more upheaval when, in 1624, her husband died at the age of 34 and she became Dowager Countess of Dorset, but not for long, for, whether she felt vulnerable as a lone mother of two girls or whatever, she married Philip Herbert, Earl of Montgomery and Pembroke. Again, she became mistress of a great house, Wilton, which Inigo Jones was restoring. Lady Anne can be seen in the Van Dyke family group hanging in the Double Cube room there.

All this time, Anne never renounced her claim to the northern lands, and in 1641, her uncle, Francis, 4th Earl of Cumberland died, leaving his only son to become the fifth Earl. Two years later, in 1643, he too died, without issue, and, at last, nearly forty years after her father's death, the Clifford estates became hers.

During this time, the Civil War was raging in England and it wasn't until 1649 that Lady Anne set out north to her ancestral lands, arriving in Skipton where she had been born, 44 years after she left there.

In 1650, while she was away, her second husband died and she became the Dowager Countess of Pembroke. Her initials, AP, can be seen on many of the buildings she set about restoring in Westmorland. It might be thought that having gained her patrimony at 60 years of age, after such a long struggle and with little help from both husbands, she would not live much longer or have much spirit for anything. Not so.

She set about rebuilding churches and castles and, in the time of the Republic, incurred the displeasure of Lord Protector Cromwell who disapproved of such conspicuous displays of wealth. When told of this, it is claimed that Lady Anne said, 'If Cromwell knocks them down again, I shall spend my last penny rebuilding them'. She hadn't submitted to King James I and she wasn't going to do so to Cromwell.

Rebuffing the entreaties of her kin to take it easy at her age, and, like a queen making a royal progress, Lady Anne would visit her properties in a horse-litter, having sent a state bed ahead of her. If she stayed as a guest anywhere, she would leave as a gift one of her state locks.

Pendragon, Brough, Brougham and Appleby castles were returned to their previous glory. Amongst others, the churches of Skipton, Outhgill, Brough and Brougham were restored, as was St Lawrence's in Appleby where she herself was to be buried next to the tomb of her mother. Ever mindful of her duty to the poor and needy, she built almshouses for them, such as St Anne's Hospital in Appleby.

Lady Anne Clifford who had been Countess of Dorset and of Montgomery and Pembroke, a woman who had defied two rulers of England in order to hold onto what was rightfully hers, died when she was 86 on 22nd March 1676 in Brougham Castle, a Clifford stronghold, in a room where her father had been born, a fitting place for a proud, northern lady to end her days. At her funeral, Bishop Rainbow said…

'… thus died a great wise woman… fitter for an History than a sermon.'

It was well worth getting off the train to make the acquaintance of Anne Clifford, a feisty lady.

FITZROY

FITZROY

Church Road, Upper Norwood, in the south-east London borough of Croydon, must have looked grand in its day. Long and straight, it stretches from its junction with South Norwood Hill in the west to where it meets Crystal Palace Parade in the east. It still has many of the houses which made it one of the grandest and most historic roads in this conservation area.

In its past it has seen some distinguished inhabitants and visitors: Queen Victoria stayed at the hotel named after her when opening the Crystal Palace nearby; the Kaiser, too, visited that marvel of the age and stayed at the hotel named after his grandmother; Emile Zola stayed there for almost a year after fleeing France when he was sentenced to imprisonment for defending Alfred Dreyfus and here he indulged his other passion besides writing, photography, and took great pleasure in recording the life and environs of the area. The poet Walter de la Mare lived on Church Road, as did the film director Ken Russell who, according to local legend, used to pop round to the shops in Westow Street in his bare feet.But, perhaps, one of the most distinguished, yet not widely known, inhabitants of this, in its day, dignified road, was Admiral Robert FitzRoy (and, please note, he always insisted on spelling his name this way, definitely not 'Fitzroy').

Those of us who wake early and, rather than get out of bed, often turn on the radio and dozily listen to the 05:20 Shipping Forecast, must have been surprised on the morning of February 4th, 2002 to find 'Finisterre' missing, to be replaced by a new nomenclature for that sea area to the west of 'Biscay' and between 'Sole' and 'Trafalgar': it is now called 'Fitzroy'. What's this? we must have thought.

Robert FitzRoy (1805-1865) came from an aristocratic family and was a great grandson of King Charles II. His grandfather was the Duke of Grafton and his mother the daughter of the Marquess of Londonderry. Such a pedigree did not hinder his progress in his chosen career in the navy where he established his reputation as a surveyor and commander. His most famous command was that of HMS Beagle.

Admiral FitzRoy is buried in the churchyard of All Saints Church, Upper Norwood, not far from his last home on Church Road. On the headstone of his grave are biographical details, plus those of his wife, and three quotations from the Bible, but no mention is made of the fact that he was Captain of the Beagle during its voyage round the South American coast and the Galapagos Islands with Charles Darwin who became the ship's naturalist and, as a result, wrote 'On The Origin of Species by Means of Natural Selection' (published 1859), a book which changed history and scientific thought. Neither is there mention that he was Governor-General and Commander-in-Chief of New Zealand, a post, one would imagine, to be proud of. Strange omissions.

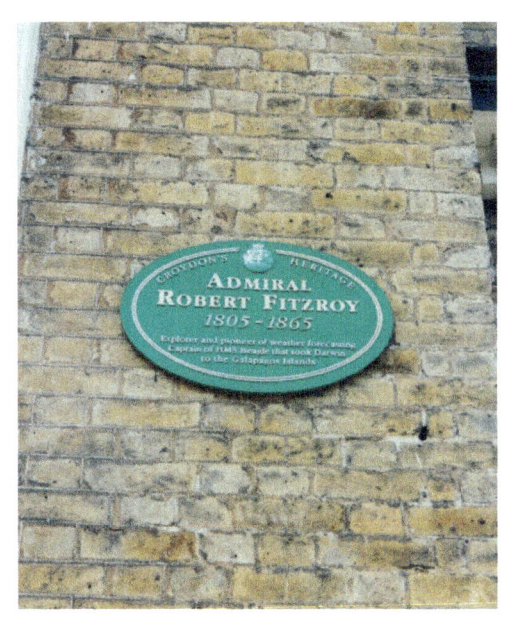

The plaque on FitzRoy's home, in Church Road, Upper Norwood.

In the Church of All Saints is this picture of HMS Beagle in Tahiti

At the foot of the grave is another stone which records that he was the first head of the Meteorological Office and devised the system of weather forecasts and storm warnings which were the prototypes of the present-day systems. He did this despite opposition from some Members of Parliament who thought that weather forecasting was akin to casting the runes and greeted the request for the funding of a meteorological department as part of the Board of Trade with derision and laughter. There was also some opposition from those who owned the fishing fleets, for they thought that forecasts of storms would prevent their boats and men from putting to sea and thereby affect their profits. And this was despite the fact that in 1859 alone, a total of 1,645 lives were lost off our coasts. The time was ripe for a weather forecast and the first appeared in '*The Times*' on August 1st, 1861, and merely said, 'General weather probable during next two days'. Needless to say that sailors and fishermen thought well of him. He had a continuing interest in their welfare and became secretary of the Lifeboat Association for which he worked assiduously. Obviously, from the inscriptions, his family were proud enough of these achievements but why have others been omitted?

Perhaps part of the answer may lie in the fact of his erstwhile friend and shipboard companion's achievement. Fitzroy himself had recruited Darwin and they became friends, which is just as well when you think what close quarters they were to inhabit on a five year journey around the world making navigational and scientific discoveries. The previous captain of the Beagle, Pringle Stokes, had committed suicide, as had FitzRoy's uncle, the Foreign

Secretary, Viscount Castlereagh, so no doubt, he was glad to find a suitable gentleman to share the voyage with and to help alleviate the loneliness of command.

The friendship was not without its ups and downs, for FitzRoy had such a violent temper that the crew had given him the nickname 'Hot Coffee' and there were occasions when the two fell out, only for the captain to apologise and invite the young naturalist back to his table where they would discuss the scientific interests they had in common, such as Lyell's *'Principles of Geology'*.

During the Beagle's second voyage, it seems that FitzRoy was torn between the discoveries being made by his young companion and the conclusions to be drawn from them which, added to the questioning of the Scriptures implicit in Lyell's book, caused him to doubt his own faith in the biblical account of creation. However, as with many reactionaries, accepting new theories was a step too far for him and he retreated into a greater commitment to a literal reading of the Bible, for example arguing that discovery of sea shells on mountain tops was proof of the Flood and the story of Noah and his ark, and that creation could not have taken aeons because vegetation would have died for lack of sunlight during the long nights. No doubt, having returned home after such a long voyage, during which there was no theological disagreement with Darwin (though the seeds may have been sown), he fell under the influence of his very religious wife.

It was not until the publication of *'The Origin of Species'* which he claimed gave him the 'acutest pain' for the part he had played in the development of Darwin's theory, that might explain the absence of his captaincy of the Beagle from his tombstone. Such was his rejection of it that during a debate at Oxford when 'Soapy' Sam Wilberforce, Bishop of Oxford was attacking Darwin and his theory, Fitzroy 'a grey-haired, Roman-nosed elderly gentleman' stood with a Bible above his head and asked those present 'to believe in God rather than man.'

FitzRoy was an explorer before he met Darwin; he had helped to chart the southern seas and map such places as Tierra del Fuego on a previous voyage in 1839 and had brought back not only Fuegian Indians but seeds and plants for collectors and propagation purposes. He gave his name to a rare conifer, 'FitzRoya cupressoides' which can live for thousands of years. It was on the return trip to South America that Darwin accompanied him. While Darwin's 'The Voyage of the Beagle' is read and remembered, it is not well-known that this was a three volume work, the first two books of which were written by Fitzroy. His work as a surveyor was such that it was referred to in the House of Commons as 'the splendid work of Captain Robert FitzRoy'. In 1837 he was awarded the gold medal of the Royal Geographical Society.

In 1843 he was appointed first Governor General and Commander-in-Chief of New Zealand, a position which had many difficulties, for he arrived at time when there was considerable friction over land claims. The settlers expected FitzRoy to support them but he was a highly-principled man and contended that the Maoris' claims were as valid as the settlers. This did not make him popular with them. He fell out, too, with the New Zealand

The grave of Admiral Fitzroy in the graveyard of All Saints church, Upper Norwood, London.

Company over financial policy and eventually, in 1845, after much agitation by the settlers, he was recalled. This could account for the omission of such a prestigious position from his tombstone.

FitzRoy was what we call today, bi-polar, suffering all his life from bouts of melancholia and given to outbursts of ferocious temper. Eventually, on 30th April 1865, depression, failing health and financial worries caused him to take his life.

He died having exhausted his fortune and when this became known, a fund was started to support his family. Queen Victoria gave them a grace and favour apartment at Hampton Court Palace and Darwin was one of the many who contributed to the fund, giving £100, a huge sum in those days.

A plaque has been placed on his home in Church Road which records that he was 'Explorer and pioneer of weather forecasting, and captain of the Beagle that took Darwin to the Galapagos Islands'. How would he have responded to this last tribute, I wonder, but I'm sure that having a shipping area named after him which is heard regularly by thousands of mariners and contributes to their safety would please him no end.

HE BEING DEAD, YET
SPEAKETH

HE BEING DEAD, YET SPEAKETH

Many men will tell you that their barber's shop is the best 'Gentlemen's Club' going-newspapers, amiable company, good chat and no sign of 'her indoors'. Great, until he moved to the country, mine was no different.

Eric Price's barber shop at 84 Anerley Road in southeast London was always good for a 'number three all over, please, Eric' and we'd natter away, putting the world to rights. One day as I sat in the chair, he said, 'I'm mongrel Welsh, you know, Taff.'

'Really, Eric?'

'Yes, on my mother's side. We're mentioned in '*Kilvert's Diary*'. And he went upstairs, for he then lived over the shop, and brought down the Folio Society three volume edition of the diary. And there they were, the Price family, unfortunately referred to as 'rogues and cattle thieves'. This serendipitous beginning was my introduction to this delightful work.

English literature has a number of diaries which became famous long after the authors' deaths: John Evelyn (1620-1706) gives us a vivid picture of the Restoration Court of Charles II and his own troubles with Peter the Great, Czar of Muscovy to whom he had let his house, Sayes Court in Deptford, in his diary which was found in an old clothes basket after his death; Samuel Pepys (1633-1703) another, perhaps more famous diarist, wrote his diary in code, telling us not only of the Plague and the Great Fire of London, but also of his own somewhat saucy peccadilloes and the work was not deciphered until 1825, a hundred and twelve years after he died.

In 1938-40, the writer William Plomer edited the diaries, almost sixty years after his death, of Francis Kilvert, a clergyman who lived from 1840-1879 and they received great acclaim for the detailed picture he drew of mid-Victorian times, especially the rural lives of the Marches, that frontier region of England and Wales, the borderland of Radnorshire and Herefordshire.

Kilvert was born in Wiltshire, the son of a vicar, and was educated privately before going up to Wadham College, Oxford. After his ordination in Bristol Cathedral in 1864 he became his father's curate for a while before, in 1865, he went to Clyro in Radnorshire to become curate at the church of St Michael and all Angels from 1865-1872.

It was the years he spent in the parishes of this area of the Black Mountains and the Wye Valley that were his happiest. The wild, remote uplands and the gentle river valleys enchanted Kilvert and inspired him to keep a diary for, as he said, he didn't think a life as dull and uninteresting as his should pass without a record.

With one exception, when he returned to Wiltshire for a short time to be his father's curate again, he lived the rest of his brief life in the Marches, first in the living of St Harmon, near Rhayader, in Wales and then as Vicar of Bredwardine, back in England. It was during the last ten years of his life that he kept the diary that made him posthumously famous and that attracts fans from all over the world to follow the Kilvert Trail to those places and churches associated with him.

He took great interest in the life and work of the great Romantic poet, William Wordsworth and like him, he too was a keen observer of the life around him. He describes his natural surroundings, the rise and fall of the seasons, the changes in the foliage, flowers and weather, not to mention the associated agricultural customs, whether it be Harvest

Sitting on Kilvert's bench.

Thanksgiving Super or the embarrassment he felt when he saw a clergyman's daughter helping to castrate lambs.

His religious beliefs and the beauty of his surroundings inspired him to write poetry as well but his verse doesn't have the vitality and immediacy of his diary though a selection of it was printed privately three years after his death and called *'Musings in Verse'*.

Kilvert had an affinity with the plain country folk who were his parishioners and we meet colourful characters as he goes about 'villaging', as he called his pastoral visits, a duty he performed conscientiously. One such memorable member of his flock was 'the old soldier', John Morgan. who lived to the great age of 97. He had fought in the Peninsular Wars against Napoleon's forces and Kilvert often listened to his exploits.

He visited the more well-to-do also, lunching with the Bishop of Hereford, dining with the local gentry, attending balls and playing croquet, so there was social diversity in his life which is recorded in his journals.

His diary is not without humour. Once in a village school where he taught, he asked the class what an embalmed Egyptian body was called. 'A muffin', answered a child.

Local catastrophes did not pass him by and he tells of floods which devastated farms and villages, carrying away livestock and ruining homes. National tragedies are mentioned also, such as the collision in the River Thames between the *'Princess Alice'*, an excursion steamer, and *'The Bywell Castle'*, a collier, in which 700 people died.

While he loved his country parish, he wasn't a 'stay-at home' and travelled to Liverpool, Cornwall, the Isle of

In the churchyard at St Andrew's Church, Bredwardine.

The Rev. Francis Kilvert MA – a portrait in the church at Clyro.

He Being Dead, Yet Speaketh 111

Wight and a number of times to London where he enjoyed visiting the Dulwich Picture Gallery and, especially, the nearby Crystal Palace where once he attended the Handel Festival where he arrived a little too late for a good seat but enjoyed it enormously, nevertheless.

He gives us other details of his private life, telling of a painful attack of 'emerods' which laid him up for a few days. Once, on a visit to Bath, he had two teeth 'stopped' and bought six pairs of kid gloves.

Kivert had an affectionate nature and a number of romantic attachments. Daisy Thomas, daughter of the vicar of St Elgen's, Llanigon, a nearby parish, was one of them and when he asked her father permission to court her, the Rev. Thomas forbade it because Kilvert had poor prospects. A poignant insight into this was gained in future years, long after Kilvert's death, when Daisy, still single in old age, was asked why she had never married, replied: 'No one ever asked me but I think Mr. Kilvert liked me.' Touching, that.

It was on holiday in Paris in 1877 that he met Elizabeth Ann Rowland from Oxfordshire and in 1879 they married. After a honeymoon in Scotland they returned to Bredwardine where, a little over a month after their wedding, Francis died of peritonitis at the age of 39. His wife, having removed all references to her, kept the diary for the rest of her life until, on her death, it passed to her husband's nephew, Perceval Smith who in arranging for its publication gave to the world what John Betjeman called 'the best picture of vicarage life in Victorian England'. On Kilvert's tombstone are inscribed the words, 'He being dead, yet speaketh' and when we read his diary we realise how true this is.

So you see, much can be gained from a chat in the barber's chair.

MARTYRS

MARTYRS

If I'd known that A Level English was going to entail all this research, perhaps I'd have had second thoughts. It wasn't the Donne and the Shakespeare that I'd found time-consuming but Hardy's 'Tess of the D'Urbervilles', my 'special' topic, that was giving me gyp. Like everyone else, I found Alec a creep, an oily cad, but it was Angel Clare's piousness that got on my wick. I wanted to put my boot up his rustic bum and say, 'Go on, give her a second chance.' Of course, then there would have been no story but still, I thought it. And then when 'Hoppy', my English teacher suggested a trip to Hardy country, little did I suspect I'd be confused by the place names.

Turnerspuddle, Briantspuddle, Affpuddle, Piddletrenthide, and Puddleton: what is it with all these 'piddles' and 'puddles'? And isn't there one missing? Well, all these villages can be found in Dorset in the valley of the small rural River Piddle which rises in Alton Pancras and runs, after a little over 24 miles, into Poole Harbour. Like its more famous neighbours the Stour and Frome, it is a chalk stream and gets its name from the Anglo-Saxon word 'piddle' which means 'a boggy or marshy place'. No doubt, Alfred the Great, the founder of the Kingdom of Wessex of which Dorset forms a part, had subjects who fished its gently-flowing, pellucid waters, as do fishermen today, many of whom come for their sport to the trout stocked lakes of Tollpuddle. Ah, that's the missing 'puddle', and the one that is world famous for more than just trout fishing.

Tolpuddle (called Tolchurch in Thomas Hardy's *'Desperate Remedies'*) lies on the A35 between Bournemouth and Dorchester but since the new by-pass has been built much of the traffic has been diverted, leaving the village with its thatched roofs and lush meadows much quieter.

However, in 1831, Tolpuddle saw the start of a movement which not only made 6 of its menfolk 'martyrs', but went on to become of worldwide significance. In order, as they said 'to save their wives and children from utter degradation and starvation', six farm labourers met under a sycamore tree on the village green and decided to bond together to ask for a rise in wages. They were getting 7 shillings (35p) a week and they asked for 10 shillings (50p). Not only did they not get an increase but their wages were reduced.

Over the next three years they met their employers a number of times and repeated their request but to no avail. There was no violence and nothing was destroyed. They were Christian men who were trying to escape from rural poverty and agricultural depression.

The squire, James Frampton, like many landowners, was alarmed by their demands, as was the Whig government which saw working-class discontent all over the country. The masters thought the social fabric of the nation was at risk if the 'have nots', like Oliver Twist, asked for more and

Outside the Martyrs' Museum is this modern memorial to the martyrs.

in 1834 the six men were arrested. The Loveless brothers, George and James (both of whom were Methodist lay preachers), James Brine, Thomas Standfield and his son John, and James Hammett were taken to Dorchester jail. They were brought to court before a hostile judge and jury made up of local landowners who had a vested interest in maintaining the status quo. The Loveless brothers had established a lodge of 'The Friendly Society of Agricultural Labourers' and they were charged as a secret society with administering an unlawful oath.

They were found guilty and sentenced to 7 years transportation to a penal colony in Australia where conditions were no better than the prison hulks where they had been kept and the convict ships which took them to the other side of the world. They were sold for £1 a head to masters as bad, and worse, than those they had left behind.

But the Government had underestimated popular sentiment. There was public outcry and large-scale demonstrations against the harsh treatment of the labourers. After nationwide protest, two years later they were given a free pardon but not before they had suffered hellish conditions in Australia. They returned home to England as heroes but not long after all, except one of them, James Hammett, emigrated to Canada. However, the right to collective bargaining, a foundation stone in the development of workers' rights and Trade Unionism, had been established.

The Martyrs' suffering and sacrifice is still recognised. Each year in July, politicians and trade unionists from all over the world march to the old sycamore on the village green. In 1934 the Trades Union Congress built six Martyrs Memorial Cottages, each named after one of the men. There is a Museum which, using interactive exhibits and illustrative displays, presents the Martyrs' story. A memorial arch has been erected outside the Methodist chapel and in the village churchyard of St John's, James Hammett's grave can be found.

A festival is held with banners flying, speeches made and lots of music and fun and games, most of which take place on the green outside the Martyrs' Cottages. Tony Benn, Dennis Skinner and other British politicians have spoken and there are representatives from countries where union activity is not easy. In London, Ontario, Canada, on September 15th, 2011 a statue to the Martyrs was unveiled in the Peace Gardens, further commemorating the doctrine of strength through unity for which the Dorset labourers fought and suffered.

When he was sentenced to penal servitude in Australia George Loveless, a Methodist lay preacher, wrote:-

'God is our guide, from field, from wave,
From plough, from anvil, and from loom;
We come, our country's rights to save,
And speak a tyrant faction's doom:
We raise the watch-word liberty;
We will, we will, we will be free.'

I'll drink to that.

Sometimes it is easy to forget that rights we take for granted were won by the likes of such men. As one who has benefitted from union membership, I too salute the Tolpuddle Martyrs and, although long-retired, continue to belong to the same union that supported and protected me when in need.

PINK SATIN LIPS

PINK SATIN LIPS

Some of you may remember that in a previous book, 'London Lives', I recounted how, in the National Gallery in Trafalgar Square, I was asked to move out of the way because I was 'standing on Greta Garbo', a mosaic on the main staircase. I don't want you to think that I'm a philistine or iconoclast but a similar thing happened with Mae West's lips some time ago. But, let's go back to the beginning.

In September 2010, I think it was, Pallant House Gallery in Chichester had an exhibition *'Surreal Friends'* and in the Queen Anne townhouse where the museum began, there was a complementary show, *'Surrealism in Sussex'*. Many people thought that the title itself was surreal enough, not realising that the county had connections with that art movement. Roland Penrose, a Sussex resident, artist, collector and organiser of the International Surrealist Exhibition in London in 1936, was influential in getting the works of the surrealists more well-known. And in nearby West Dean lived the poet and collector Edward James who at one time had one of the largest collections of surreal art in the world.

Anyway, at the exhibition there were paintings and objects such as Dali's lobster phones (two of them) and his three Mae West's lips sofas, one of which was in pink satin.

We'd shared a moment together, that sofa and I. It was when I'd gone with an old school chum to the flint-faced manor house at the centre of James's West Dean Estate for a literary weekend. We were making our way, early, to the lecture room when, lo and behold, there in the corridor was this slightly faded but nonetheless icon of surrealism, a sofa in the shape of Mae West's lips. Of course, you can guess what I did. I sat on it, dear reader. Well, wouldn't you?

'There's a notice here that says do not sit on this sofa,' said Colin who hated fuss and usually toed the line. 'You'd better get off it.'

So I did. Now the sofa has been transferred upstairs and is in a big glass case, safe from bottoms such as mine.

West Dean, in the beautiful Sussex countryside, was the home of Edward James (1907-1981), a colourful and eccentric character. Novelist, poet, and art collector with enough money to indulge his passions, he became friend and patron to artists such as Salvador Dali and Rene Magritte. One of the latter's best known works *'La Reproduction Interdite'* is that of a slim young man looking into a mirror in which all we can see is the back of his head. It is a portrait (?) of Edward James.

He inherited the estate in 1912, from his father, when he was four and at his coming of age he set about investing time and money in giving support to all kinds of artists, craftsmen, poets (he was the first to publish John Betjeman) and dancers. In fact, his marriage to one of the latter, Tilly Losch, who was three years older than him, was not a success and when they parted she said he was a homosexual and he, unsportingly by the mores of the times, accused

West Dean.

West Dean – church and manor house.

her of adultery. A gentleman didn't do such things and he was shunned by many society 'friends'. The divorce was messy, expensive and a host of celebrities were witnesses, including Sir Thomas Beecham and Randolph Churchill. A lasting legacy of their union can still be seen at West Dean where there is a staircase covered with a carpet that bears the damp imprints of her bare feet as she emerged from the bath: this was a gift that James had made for her. The carpet lasted longer than the marriage and Tilly went on to marry the Earl of Caernarvon. She left him after ten weeks.

It wasn't only the James's marriage and divorce that was notorious. Edward's lineage was a cause for question also. Although in youth he was slim, as he aged he grew to look remarkably like King Edward VII, a frequent visitor to West Dean and a monarch known for his eye for the ladies. Some clever clogs good at sums put together a weekend that the king was on the James' estate with the fact that almost exactly nine months later an heir was born to Willie and his attractive young wife who were the king's hosts. Hanging on one of the corridor walls is a photograph showing Edward James in middle age which adds weight to this tale. He looks remarkably like the king. Whatever the truth of the matter, William James accepted Edward as his own son. Was there any significance in the choice of name for the boy, I wonder?

The major part of the rest of Edward's life post-Tilly was spent abroad. At first, he went to Italy where at the Villa Cimbrone in Ravello he settled for a while before, at the beginning of World War II, he moved to America. He lived in California for the next 25 years, mainly in Los Angeles, in Hollywood, where he met Aldous Huxley and, like many others, came under the influence of the Indian theosophist, Jiddu Krishnamurti.

His eccentricities continued: his obsessive/compulsive behaviour showed itself in his habit of packing everything he had wherever he went in pink tissue paper. He even packed the tissue paper in tissue paper which caused puzzlement to one custom's officer. Edward loved animals and once, at a hotel, when a guest complained of mice, the manager told her they were for Mr. James's boa-constrictors which were accompanying him on his travels. Flowers were his other great love. At one time he had 27,000 varieties of orchid.

Perhaps flowers were the main reason he indulged his last great passion and moved to Mexico to build his second memorable legacy to the world, Las Pozas, his fantasy in the jungle near Xilitla. Here he built fantastic structures, gigantic columns shaped like flowers, huge concrete platforms over which the jungle spread its tentacles and strange sub-tropical vegetation. And, of course, the nine pools which give the place its name stretched out along the river in which the local people came to swim. Fortunately, since his death in 1981, Las Pozas has been taken over by the State and is managed as a national treasure.

His first great legacy and the one with which this story started was the Edward James Foundation which he set up in 1964 and which opened West Dean College to nurture music, arts and crafts. To study and train, whether on a short course or long, in such a beautiful place is a privilege indeed and one for which many of us are grateful. I may no longer be able to plonk my ageing buttocks on Mae West's pink satin lips and thereby connect with Salvador Dali and the Surrealists, but in the bar I can lift a glass to the memory of Edward James, creator of beautiful things.

SNOTTY-GOGS AND PONTIUS PILATE

SNOTTY-GOGS AND PONTIUS PILATE

'Old age doesn't come alone, my lad'. I remember an old friend saying as we hacked our way through a bosket. And, boy, was he right. Since getting my Freedom Pass, a great liberator, I've found out the wisdom of those words. In an effort not to ossify, I've joined a couple of walking groups. Kill two birds with one stone, I thought, some exercise and a bit of company. So, now, two mornings each week I set out heartily (it doesn't last) through the Surrey countryside.

It's surprising what you pick up on these strolls. One day, when in Tandridge, a Surrey parish popular with walkers, a companion told me to go and have a look at the church, St Peter's, I might find it interesting, especially the tower and one or two of the graves. So, at the end (thank the Lord) of one walk, I foreswore the pleasure of a pint and went to the church instead.

I did indeed find the church of some interest. It is described in Kelly's Directory as 'an ancient building of stone in the Decorated style'. The bell tower with its shingle spire is most attractive, especially as the church is in an elevated position and the tower acts as a beacon and fixed point for miles around. Unfortunately, it was locked so I couldn't get in to see 'the Decorated style' and Sir Giles Gilbert Scott's additions.

I did find something of interest in the churchyard and it wasn't one of the graves. It was an enormous yew, massive thing, which towers over the church. As I made my way around its huge trunk, the weak October light was having difficulty getting through the palm-like leaves laden with scarlet berries. I stooped to pick up a few which had fallen.

'They're poisonous,' came a voice from the ether before its owner appeared from the other side of the enormous trunk.

'I've seen birds eat them,' I said.

'Yes but only some birds. Thrushes, great tits and green finches eat them without any harmful effect. They're poisonous to men and animals. Try one if you don't believe me.'

'Think I'll give it a miss,' I said, looking round at the churchyard. 'The place is full up anyway.'

The unknown gent turned out to be a parishioner visiting his wife's grave. He seemed to know a lot about the tree.

'It's the second biggest yew in England. Its girth is 34 feet. And it's one of the oldest. Some say it's 2,500 years old.'

'That's not only older than this church, it's older than the Church itself.'

Eventually, after more arboreal chat, he wandered off to tidy up his missus's grave and I was left reflecting on yews.

The yew (*taxus baccata*) is usually associated with graveyards. Some pre-Christian tribes revered the tree and after victorious battles would hang as trophies in the boughs not only their defeated enemies' shields but also their heads. As well as the oak, the Druids held the yew sacred too and planted them in or near their temples. The ground was therefore consecrated when Christian missionaries arrived and seen as suitable sites for places of worship. Ancient yews predated not only their neighbouring churches but Christianity itself.

Yews grow in many countries in the Northern Hemisphere. In the British Isles it has many names: in Welsh it is 'ywen'; in Irish, 'iur' ; in Gaelic, 'iubahr' ;and in some places in south-east England its fronds were carried in the Palm Sunday procession before the now more familiar palm fronds were available.

They are slow-growing trees and although they grow in a number of habitats, they can especially occur on neutral or alkaline soils. Many grow in the New Forest and there is a 360 acre wood at Kingley Vale in Hampshire. One method of propagation occurs when the main branches of very old trees, often hollow, touch the ground and take root, a process called layering. The more common method is when pollen from the catkin-like flowers of the male tree is wind-borne, usually in February, to the green flowers of the female. By October, these have become scarlet berries (known as 'snotty-gogs' in some parts of the country), which are poisonous, as I was told, to men and animals though some birds, as aforementioned, can eat them without harm. The seed inside the berry can lie dormant for as long as eighteen months before putting forth leaves.

The sapwood of the yew is pale and thin, the heartwood rust-red. It is a wood favoured by woodturners and furniture makers because it can make attractive veneers. Because it is hard and durable, it has been used as posts, fences and gates, often outlasting more conventional iron and steel. Viking longships were often built with yew as nails. Some wine barrels are made from yew, as are domestic utensils such as trenchers and bowls. It is a useful tree for topiary and in hedges: on Lord Bathurst's estate in Cirencester in Gloucestershire there is a famous yew hedge planted in 1720 which is 35 feet high and 120 yards long. At Aberglasney gardens, a Tudor relic, in West Wales, there is a yew tunnel which is claimed to be a thousand years old. Like the London plane tree, yew is relatively immune to pollution.

There is much folk lore attached to the yew. Because of its longevity and the fact it is evergreen, it has been seen as a symbol of immortality though, because of its toxic properties and their frequent occurrence in graveyards, they have also been seen as symbols of death. Janus-like, yews face both ways, to the past and to the future.

At Fortingall in Perthshire, Scotland, there is a yew with a long history and notorious associations. It is claimed to be more than eight thousand years old and though it is now a gnarled trunk which has suffered the depredations of time, weather and vandalism, legend has it that Pontius Pilate played in its shade as a child. His father, a Roman envoy, had been sent in about 10 BC by the Emperor Augustus to collect tribute from Mainus, a local chieftain. While there, Pilate's father dallied with a local maiden and young Pontius was the result. He returned to Italy with his father, became a Roman citizen, rose through the ranks and was eventually appointed Governor of Judea. The rest we know.

Tandridge – this ancient yew towers over the parish church and has a girth of over 34 feet.

However, his story may not have ended with the washing of his hands at the trial of Jesus, for after the Crucifixion, Pilate seems to have fallen from favour and vanished. There are those who claim he returned to his mother's homeland, Scotland, and died there, so, perhaps, he not only played beneath the branches of the Fortingall yew as a boy, but he may be buried close to it. There is a site of a Roman encampment nearby and 'Fortingall' means 'fort of the strangers'. Some of the eastern orthodox churches claim that Pilate converted to Christianity so stranger things have been known than the claim that he is buried in Perthshire. Although the tree is in such a decrepit state, the Forestry Commission have taken cuttings and are cultivating them in their laboratory so, once again, the tree that may have sheltered the child who became the man responsible for Christ's death may live again: a fitting symbol for the Christian story.

There is also a tradition that the status of a buried corpse can be told by the number of yews around the grave: four trees in a square denote royalty; three a duke; and two a lord.

Yew has more verifiable history associated with it. Although it is a heavy wood, it has an elasticity that makes it suitable for military uses in such weapons as spears and bows. Near Clacton in Essex, what is claimed to be the world's oldest artefact, a yew spear, has been found which is over a hundred thousand years old.

King Henry V (1387-1422) used the English yew longbow to devastating effect in his wars against the French, especially in the Battle of Agincourt, 1415, when their army under the Duke of Orleans was defeated utterly. Edward IV (1442-1483) of the House of York proclaimed that every able-bodied Englishman should have a bow of yew or ash. His brother, 'Dick Crookback', Richard III (1452-1485) was far-sighted enough to order yew woods to be planted for the purpose of making bows in the future and was forced by their shortage at one stage to import yew staves from Spain.

Not only are yews slow-growing and long-lived but they also grow to great size. Surrey can claim to have two of the oldest and largest, the aforementioned one at Tandridge and one in the churchyard of St George's church at Crowhurst where there are a number of yews, including one that towers over the east wall. It is claimed to be the largest in England and just inside the church door there is a

Crowhurst, Surrey – the door set into the trunk of the ancient yew in the churchyard of St George's Church.

certificate signed by the then Archbishop of Canterbury, Robert Runcie, which says that 'using all the data to hand, it is estimated that the tree is 4,000 years old' and help is asked 'to maintain this venerable member of the community.'

It is measured each year on St George's Day, April 23rd, and at present is just over 33 feet in girth and its height is 45 feet with a crownspread of over 27 feet.Its centre is hollow and a door has been placed in its trunk which leads to a small room which in the past may have been used by the vestry or other church activities. At one time, before the roof caved in, it was fitted with bench seats and a table. There are claims that it was used as lock-up for local ne'er-do-wells. A cannon ball was discovered in the trunk.

So it seems that the yew has accompanied us through history, in the home, on the battlefield, as a Celtic cult and a Christian symbol. No doubt, it will continue to do so for years to come. Long live *taxus baccata*.

THE LAST PLANTAGENET?

THE LAST PLANTAGENET?

Out of curiosity, I typed in on my PC, 'Who is the most evil English monarch?' and was surprised by the result. First up was Richard I, 'Coeur de Lion', who was an absentee monarch, spending most of his reign abroad and neglecting his realm. Although thought of as a war hero, he was responsible for many thousands of deaths both in his wars in France and on the Crusades. His brother, King Henry II's third son, John, (1199-1216), surnamed 'Lackland' who was said to be 'petty, spiteful and cruel', followed. Edward I (1272-1307) was next in line not simply because he was called the Hammer of the Scots and the oppressor of the Welsh but in gaining those unenviable titles, he butchered thousands, many of whom were innocents. And finally, came Mary Tudor (1553-1558), Henry VIII's eldest daughter, whose religious hatred and prejudice brought about the death of hundreds of Protestants. I'd expected her father to put in an appearance, after all he'd had six wives, two of whom he'd divorced, two he'd had executed, one died in childbirth and the last, Katharine Parr, was lucky enough to outlive the monster.

There were others from all walks of life who suffered at his hands too. But the most glaring omission was Richard III (1483-1485) whom everyone loves to hate. After all, didn't he have his two young nephews murdered in the Tower of London and didn't he kill his brother, George? His 'motiveless malignancy' is well-known. He was an ambitious and ruthless usurper, and deformed with it. 'Dick Crookback', the malevolent ruler of England for two years is a favourite villain of many. But, perhaps, there was another side to him.

'This sceptered isle' has a long and rich history, full of incident, pomp and panoply, stretching from before the Roman invasions by Julius Caesar in 55 and 54 BC. Usually, it is those in power who are remembered but, sometimes, the less-eminent have their stories to tell.

In Kent, the Garden of England, just north of Ashford, under the North Downs and close to the Pilgrims' Way, is St Mary's Church, Eastwell, now in ruins and in the ownership of 'The Friends of Friendless Churches', a charitable company set up to look after redundant places of worship as peaceful spaces for the local community and general public to enjoy and as part of the nation's history.

St Mary's setting is romantic and evocative. It lies down a country lane, shaded by trees, beside a lily-covered Eastwell Lake, one of the largest artificial lakes in Kent, fed by the waters of the nearby River Stour.

The grounds are mostly overgrown. Trees, bushes and brambles have hidden many of the gravestones as nature reclaims her own. However, one tomb, near the mortuary chapel which still stands, is visible and accessible. It is an

In St Mary's Churchyard, Eastwell, in Kent, is this tomb with the barely legible inscription 'The reputed tomb of Richard Plantagenet, 22 December 1550.'

The ruins of St Mary's Church, Eastwell, near Ashford, Kent, where the reputed tomb of Richard Platagenet lies.

The Last Plantagenet? 145

altar tomb and on one side is the inscription: 'Reputed tomb of Richard Plantagenet 22 December 1550.'

This overgrown and weathered grave tells a fascinating story.

Richard III, King of England, 1483-1485, is one of the most reviled men in English history. Shakespeare's eponymous play and Tudor propaganda have meant that his character has been blackened: he has been accused of murdering Henry VI and his son, Edward, Prince of Wales, of poisoning his own wife Anne Neville and of killing the Princes in the Tower, Edward V and his younger brother.

In an age of political turbulence, of confusion and bloodshed, as in most ages, it is the winner who writes the history, and after Richard III's death at the Battle of Bosworth in 1485, at the age of 33, the incoming dynasty, the Tudors, with Henry VII as the first, actively discredited Richard. Even the 'saintly' Thomas More describes him as 'crookbacked, malicious and arrogant of heart', saying also that 'he spared no man's death whose life withstood his purpose.' However, his two year reign has engendered much research and controversy. There are those historians and Plantagenet camp-followers who claim he was an able ruler who made important administrative and financial reforms. And even though he was unhorsed at Bosworth Field, Holinshed in his Chronicles writes: 'He himself manfully fought in the midst of his enemies' before he was slain. He lost his life and his kingdom. His naked body was taken to Leicester for public display and then placed in an unmarked grave. Henry VII, not a man to spend money lightly, later gave ten pounds for a tomb for Richard. However, during the Dissolution of the Monasteries, it was destroyed. It is claimed that Richard's body was thrown into the river. The last monarch of the House of York had no known grave until it was discovered recently beneath a carpark in Leicester.

The story behind the reputed occupant of the tomb at St Mary's, Eastwell may show another side to this much-maligned king.

One day in 1535, Sir Thomas Moyle, who owned Eastwell Manor, was walking in his estate where he was having some work done, when he saw one of the workmen, a bricklayer, reading a book in a break for refreshment. In an age when most people, especially the working class, were unlettered, could neither read nor write, this surprised Sir Thomas. He approached the man and was further surprised to see that the book was in Latin. When asked where he had learned to read such a book, the bricklayer told him this tale.

As a child he had lived in a large house, looked after by a nurse with such love and devotion that he thought she was his mother. However, when he was seven he was sent to dwell in the house of a Latin schoolmaster where he was taught the language and other subjects fitting for a young gentleman. He was the only pupil so it must have been a lonely existence which was relieved every quarter by the appearance of a man who paid his fees and gave him pocket-money.

He stayed with the schoolmaster until he was 17 when the stranger came to fetch him for a journey. They went to a grand house where Richard, for that was his name, was left alone in a room. Shortly, another man came in. He was richly dressed and wore the Order of the Garter. He examined Richard. Eventually, the man gave the puzzled youth a bag of gold coins and he was taken back to the schoolmaster's house.

Not long after, the stranger came for the last time, telling Richard that they were going far away, to Leicestershire. So the young man left the only home he had known for many years and went to Bosworth Field where amid the gathering army he was taken to the most splendid tent, that belonging to the King, Richard III. The king embraced him and said, 'I am the king, your father. Tomorrow, I will battle with Henry Tudor, Earl of Richmond, for my throne. If I win I will acknowledge you as my son and you will be with me always but if I lose, you must forget what I have told you, for my enemies will hunt you down and kill you. Watch the battle from a safe place and if I am victorious, come to my tent. If I am not, go far away from here and remain anonymous.'

Young Richard, whose head must have been full of wonder at this news, went to a hill overlooking the battlefield and on the morrow saw the father he had known but briefly defeated. He fled to London and in an attempt to become inconspicuous was apprenticed to a bricklayer, for who would suspect a son of the blood royal to be learning a trade. Thus it was, years later, he ended up doing building work at Eastwell Manor.

Sir Thomas asked Richard if there was anything he could do for him. The bricklayer-prince asked leave to build a simple house on the estate where he could live out his days and serve the lord in any way he could. His request was granted. Richard built his modest house and remained there until he died on December 22nd 1550. He was buried, it is alleged, in the tomb at St Mary's, though it is claimed the inscription is of a later date.

Now why should not the tale of the enigmatic Richard of Eastwell be dismissed as fanciful conjecture? Well, in the parish register there is the entry:

'Rychard Plantagenet was buryed the 22 daye of December, sub anno 1550'

And near to the Manor House is a building called 'Plantagenet Cottage' which is supposed to stand on the site of Richard's home. Also, nearby is a source of water called 'Plantagenet Well': did Richard draw his water from it?

The historian Alison Weir in her book *'Britain's Royal Families: the complete Genealogy'* says that Richard III had seven illegitimate children and she names Richard of Eastwell as one of them. There are those who support this theory, for every so often, bouquets of white roses, symbol of the House of York, are placed on the tomb in this lovely corner of the English countryside.

THE LILLIE PAD

THE LILLIE PAD

Do you remember that BBC situation comedy of the 70's, '*Some Mothers Do 'ave 'em*' by Raymond Allen? It starred Michele Dotrice and Michael Crawford as her accident-prone husband, Frank Spencer, usually in a tank-top and beret. Well, worrisome offspring are not confined to the working class.

Queen Victoria was not amused by the antics of her son and heir, the Prince of Wales, Prince Albert Edward, known as Bertie. She resented and was jealous of his popularity in case it overshadowed her own. Thinking him frivolous, she kept official documents from him and allowed him no role in the affairs of state. She was appalled when in 1870 he was cited as a witness in a divorce case. No wonder he was 'frivolous'. What else could he do while waiting in the wings for 60 years for the throne but indulge his passion for good food and wine, cigars, horses, the theatre, yachts and beautiful women who, often, were married.

For a time, one of his chief 'frivolities' was Emilie Charlotte le Breton, one of the Dean of Jersey's seven children and second wife of Edward Langtry, a rich man who had provided her with the means of escape from provincial island life when his yacht sailed into St Helier harbour. Lillie herself said that when she saw the beautiful vessel she determined to become its mistress, so she married its owner. She sailed away from Jersey and into London society where her looks and the manipulative skills of a courtesan soon made her famous. She was such a beauty that she sat for many of the painters of her day: Whistler painted her, as did Sir Frederick Leighton and Sir Edward Burne-Jones but perhaps the most famous portrait of all, which gave her the name by which she became known, was the one by Millais, *'The Jersey Lily'* (now in St Helier Museum). She became one of the Pre-Raphaelite's, Professional Beauties, whose pictures could be found on cigarette cards, in the newspapers and on popular prints which were sold at one penny each. Lillie Langtry's sold the most.

Oscar Wilde became a friend, claiming to be besotted by her beauty. It was said that he slept on her doorstep and, ever the poseur, wandered the streets with a lily in his hand. William Ewart Gladstone, the Liberal prime minister, was an ardent admirer as was his opponent, another prime minister, Benjamin Disraeli. But it wasn't only the rich and famous who were beguiled by the Jersey Lily. Students waited outside theatres for her and, on one occasion, unhitched the horses and pulled her carriage home.

Her marriage was not a success. Edward Langtry wasted most of his fortune on drink and, it is claimed, after three years of married life, they slept apart. This does not mean that Lillie slept alone. She took a number of lovers, the most famous of whom was Bertie, the Prince of Wales a bon viveur and voluptuary.

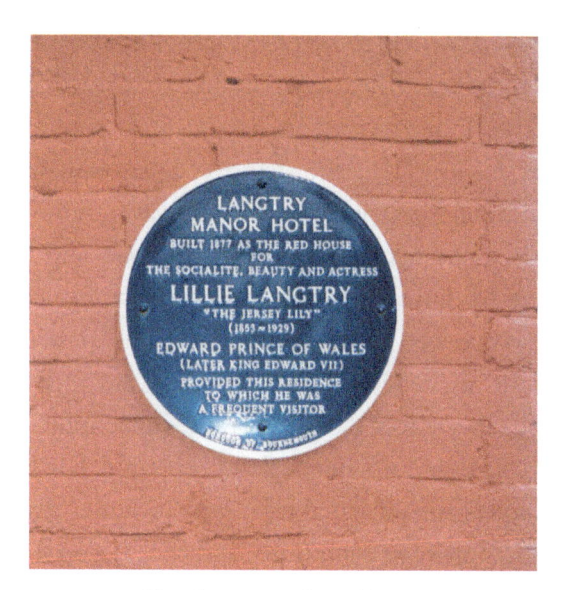

The plaque on Lillie's old home

Langtry Manor Hotel, Bournemouth – formerly 'The Red House' which Bertie, Prince of Wales, had built for his mistress, Lillie Langtry.

On May 25 1877, Sir Allen Young, a member of the Prince's circle, was asked to invite her to a small, exclusive dinner party. Lillie records in her book of reminiscences, *'The Days I Knew'* that the Prince was late and when he arrived and they were introduced, she was tongue-tied and shy. This is to be taken with a pinch of salt and was, I'm sure, a ploy to draw the would-be king into her coils. It is said that whenever alone with a man she desired, Lillie would 'faint' in order to be caught by the unsuspecting fellow and, in such a close embrace, she could begin to draw him further into her web by opening her beautiful blue eyes into his concerned face. At that dinner party, Lillie and Bertie sat next to each other and thus began a two and a half year affair when she became the mistress of the future king and emperor.

In some respects they were two of a kind: they both loved life and the pleasures of the flesh. Bertie indulged her. In 1877, amidst the pine trees on Bournemouth's East Cliff, he built for her 'The Red House', a mock-Tudor retreat where they could be together away from London, the court and all the gossip attendant upon their relationship. Today it is a prize-winning hotel, 'The Langtry Manor', licensed to perform civil marriages and which contains many signs of its most famous occupants among its up-to-date, attractive decor. The King's Room still has a four-poster bed. Around the fireplace are the beautiful gold-leaf tiles showing scenes and characters from Shakespeare's plays. On the landing is the peephole through which, unknown to his guests below, Bertie would inspect them to see if they were interesting enough to join for dinner. Perhaps most significant of all is the motto which Lillie had painted on the minstrel's gallery, 'They say-What say they?-Let them say.' She was a woman of independent mind and though she may have scandalised Victorian society, she didn't care.

Lillie was the first of Bertie's many mistresses to be publicly acknowledged. She was even presented to Queen Victoria and befriended by his wife, the long-suffering Danish Princess Alexandra. If Bertie had many mistresses, so too did Lillie have other lovers beside the Prince of Wales. One of them was his own nephew, Prince Louis of Battenburg, by whom, in 1880, Lillie became pregnant. It is claimed that this was the reason that the Prince began to distance himself from her. Others say that Lillie became too familiar with him in public, on one occasion dropping ice down his back at a dinner party. He was not amused. Perhaps it was just his libidinous nature. Whatever, he soon moved on to another Professional Beauty, Daisy, Countess of Warwick, and from her to the Honourable Mrs. Alice Keppel who remained his mistress till he died. Such was Queen Alexandra's charitable nature that she even called her to his deathbed.

Even though Bertie and Lillie drifted apart, they remained good friends to the end. He sent a gift to her daughter when she married. Lillie took to the stage and formed her own theatrical company which successfully toured the United States and the United Kingdom. Her acting was wooden but people didn't pay to see that, they came to see the beautiful woman who had beguiled a king and became his mistress.

She had further lovers, rich, famous and powerful men.

Edward Langtry refused to divorce her and it wasn't until he died that she married a man many years her junior, Hugo de Bathe who became a baronet at his father's death. Lillie became Lady de Bathe. She retired to her villa, 'Le Lys' in Monaco where she survived in style, visiting England occasionally and even having tea at Buckingham Palace with Bertie's son, King George V. She died on February 12th 1929, nineteen years after the death of her most famous lover. Her body was taken back to St Helier for burial in St Saviour's churchyard. The Jersey Lily had come home.

THE SHROPSHIRE
PIRATE

THE SHROPSHIRE PIRATE

Sport and me never got on. People think that because I'm a Taffy I must play rugby for Wales, sing all the time and swig beer like there's no tomorrow. All wrong. 'What about school?' They ask. 'Didn't you do games at school?' No, I didn't. I had a very enlightened PE teacher who had got so used to my pathetic attempts to avoid climbing ropes, jumping over boxes and other, to me, pointless and boring activities that he thought up the most marvellous punishment. 'Well', he said one day when my gym kit was in the wash yet again, 'you can learn some poetry. What are you studying in English at the moment?'

'Coleridge's *'Ancient Mariner'*, sir.'

'Learn fifty lines of that. And you can recite it to me later.'

'Bliss,' I thought, and got stuck into it while my classmates climbed, jumped and generally got sweaty. Ugh! And so was brought to my attention one of Shrewsbury's lesser-known sons.

Lying in a loop of the River Severn, Shrewsbury, with a population of over 70,000 is the county town of Shropshire, on the border between England and Wales. It is well-known for its flower show, its historic buildings, many of them timber-framed, the medieval abbey, Norman castle and a wealth of museums and churches. It could also lay claim to an association with one of its lesser-known offspring.

Shrewsbury has many famous sons, Clive of India, Wilfred Owen, Sir Philip Sidney, soldier and poet, Charles Darwin, Judge Jeffries, the 'Hanging Judge' and George Shelvocke, a shady character with a connection with one of the most well-known English poems.

Shelvocke, from a Shropshire farming family, was christened at St Mary's church on April 1st 1675. By the time he died, 62 years later, he'd become known not only as a successful privateer but also as one who wrote about his adventures on the high seas in a bestselling book.

In 1680, when he was fifteen, George joined the Royal Navy. He wasn't press-ganged, he joined freely and saw service in Britain's wars with Spain and France. His naval career was a success and he rose to become second lieutenant of the flagship commanded by Admiral John Benbow in the West Indies. However, like many other demobbed sailors, when the wars finished he ended up with no job, living in poverty.

In 1719, his luck changed and he became captain of the *'Speedwell'* which, along with the *'Success'* was given permission to loot Spanish ships; that's what a privateer was, a licensed pirate, one who could capture and loot enemy ships and keep the profits. The two ships were to operate along the west coast of South America but Shelvocke, under cover of a storm, broke away from the *'Success'* whose master, Captain John Clipperton had seniority which Shelvocke resented and he avoided contact with him for

*The skulls and crossbones on the pillars at the entrance to St Nicholas'
Church, Deptford, where George Shelvocke, the privateer (pirate) was buried.
His tomb is no longer there, assumed destroyed by bombs in the Second World
War. Some believe this is the origin of the pirate flag.*

the rest of the voyage. He didn't want Clipperton as his commodore. Perhaps Shelvocke had other plans.

After some success attacking Portuguese shipping off Brazil, Shelvocke steered for the Pacific coast where the *'Speedwell'* was wrecked on Selkirk Island (Robinson Crusoe's island). However, Captain and crew managed to make another, smaller craft and continued up the coast as far as Baja California, capturing and looting from Spanish vessels. He amassed a huge sum, about $100,000 gold coins. It is claimed that Shelvocke was the first man to report the presence of gold in the mountains and streams of California and this was many years before the Gold Rush.

He returned home to England across the Pacific Ocean, but his homecoming was not a happy one, for the shareholders of the voyage suspected that he had not been honest about his ill-gotten gains. They thought he had far more loot than he stated which he intended to keep for himself and the crew. It is claimed that he even 'fiddled' his men out of their rightful share of the spoils.

When he arrived back in England in 1772, Shelvocke was arrested and charged with piracy but he was acquitted because of lack of evidence. He certainly must have got his money from somewhere because he lived in comfort he had not previously been used to. Perhaps some of came from the book he wrote, *'A Voyage Round the World By Way of the Great South Sea'* which, while doing something to re-establish his reputation, did not go without criticism, for some of his crew disputed his account of events.

George Shelvocke died on 30th November 1742 at the age of 67 years. He was buried in the churchyard of St Nicholas' church in Deptford, south-east London, an area which had originally been a small, riverside village but after Henry VIII established the Royal Naval Dockyard there in 1513, became a flourishing Thameside town. Even Peter the Great, Czar of Muscovy, came there to study shipbuilding as part of his plans to modernise his empire. He also spent much time getting drunk and destroying property, as you do when an absolute monarch. Appropriately, the gateway-pillars to St Nicholas' are surmounted by stone skulls and crossbones, claimed to be the origin of the pirates' flag, 'The Jolly Roger.' Some credence is given to this claim for Sir Henry Morgan, the Welsh pirate and far more notorious than Shelvocke, used to sail from nearby Deptford Creek.

Shelvocke was buried in a chest tomb that stood against the east wall of the church but it has since been removed.

Why and to where no one seems to know. However, the Shropshire pirate left a more famous memorial. In his aforementioned book, he records that one of his crew, the second mate, Simon Hatley, had shot an albatross while they were rounding Cape Horn.

William Wordsworth in his 'Alfoxden Journal' records that on a walk which he took with his sister and Samuel Taylor Coleridge, they 'planned the poem of *'The Ancient Mariner'* founded on a dream' that a friend had had and that while 'much of the greatest part of the story was Mr Coleridge's, I myself suggested certain parts… I had been reading Shelvocke's '*Voyages*''. And the Poet Laureate told his friend of the killing of the albatross. We can therefore thank George Shelvocke, the pirate from Shropshire, for one of the treasures of English literature and I can thank my old school PE teacher for becoming acquainted with it. Much better than funny shaped balls!

THEY HAD NO CHOICE

THEY HAD NO CHOICE

If I may begin on a cosmological note: at the centre of the universe is not a numinous integument, a black hole or a pot of gold. There is a cat. Or, if you're a canine fan, a dog. Or whatever animal you are 'into'. If you don't believe me, ask my tabby, Bernard. He's certainly the centre of the universe where I'm looking from. Try to believe otherwise and see what happens.

On the morning of 29th July 1982 as the Household Cavalry Mounted Regiment was en-route to the Changing of the Guards ceremony at Buckingham Palace, a car-mounted nail bomb planted by the IRA exploded in Hyde Park, killing four soldiers and seven horses. Another soldier was fatally injured and nine more horses suffered horrific injuries. Among them was Sefton who had 34 wounds, including a severed jugular vein, which a soldier tried to staunch by taking off his shirt and applying pressure to the neck wound. After eight hours of surgery and many months of convalescence, during which he became world-famous, Sefton returned to duty.

During his time of recovery, he received thousands of 'Get Well', cards, presents galore, and the Royal Veterinary College was able to build a new wing, which they named after him, from the almost a million pounds of donations they received.

Sefton went on to become Horse of the Year, and in 1984 he was retired and lived at the Home of Rest for Horses with two of the other injured horses, Yeti and Echo, until he was 30. It's not for nothing that we Brits are known as a nation of animal lovers.

In his novel *'For Whom the Bell Tolls'*, the American author Ernest Hemingway (1898-1961) wrote:-

'The world is a fine place and worth fighting for.'

And, he might have added, those that do the fighting are worthy of remembrance and honour. The USA has the Purple Heart, the oldest American military decoration, established by George Washington in 1782 and awarded to those wounded in battles who have displayed conspicuous gallantry. In Britain, the Victoria Cross is the highest decoration for 'bravery in the presence of the enemy'. It was instigated by Queen Victoria in 1865 and is inscribed with the words 'For Valour'.

But what of those animals used by man in war for thousands of years? When the Romans invaded Britain in 55 and 54 BC, they found that the Celtic tribes had trained their dogs not only to attack the invading infantry but also to bite at the noses of the cavalry horses, thereby making them afraid and of little use. Did you know that 200,000 pigeons were used as messengers in World War II? Or that almost eight million horses were killed in World War I? Anyone who has seen *'War Horse'*, either the film or the play (based on Michael Morpurgo's book), will remember the lives those equines led and the strength and poignancy of the relationships between men and their horses.

Maria Dickin, founder in 1917 of the British animal welfare group The Peoples' Dispensary for Sick Animals

The Animals in War Memorial – from the war elephants of the maharajahs to the domestic cat.

was so moved and inspired by the courage shown by animals in active service in the Second World War that she persuaded the military to give medals to animals: thus the Dickin Medal came into being.

Our debt to our fellow animals was recorded in a book by the writer Jilly Cooper in 1983, *'Animals in War'*, which was republished in 2000 and was partly responsible for the memorial of the same name which was unveiled by The Princess Royal on Wednesday 24th November 2004 at Brook Gate, Park Lane. This memorial was the work of the sculptor David Backhouse and on the long, curved Portland stone walls are shown in bas-relief those animals which have seen active service for man's sake. Apart from the two bronze mules, heavily laden, which are struggling to reach a gap in the wall, there are elephants, camels, dogs and pigeons as expected, but also cats and glow-worms which gave light to read maps in the trenches. The inscription 'Animals in War' and 'They had no choice' are on one side of the wall. Beyond the gap, on the other side, is a spectral line of those animals lost in conflicts, and a bronze horse and dog which symbolise tenacity of spirit and hope for the future. It is very moving and since its unveiling has become something of a pilgrimage stop for those of us, British and foreign visitors, to visit to pay our respects to fellow animals who were used in our defence.

In the summer of 2006 the Imperial War Museum put on a very popular exhibition, 'The Animals' War,' where we could see and learn in greater detail of the part played by animals in military conflict. There was Winkle, a messenger pigeon in an aircraft that had to ditch over water. She flew back to her loft despite being wounded and covered in oil and enabled the rescue of the crew. Gustav, another pigeon, delivered the first message from the Normandy landings to Portsmouth on the English coast. They both were awarded medals.

Besides pigeons, horses and one cat, the most decorated animals have been dogs which, if they could talk would have extraordinary tales to tell. Some were even parachuted behind enemy lines. Such was the fate of a collie, Rob, part of a Special Service Unit, who was trained to act as a guard-dog to protect the men as they slept, exhausted after their dangerous missions. Rob made 20 parachute drops in Europe and North Africa and thoroughly deserved his Dickin Medal.

The Second World War was not a good time for those animals in towns that were the object of bombing raids.

A terrier being parachuted behind enemy lines – one of the exhibits at the Imperial War Museum's 'Animals at War'.

The PDSA had animal rescue squads that searched among the rubble of blitzed buildings in London for trapped animals. A wire-haired terrier named Beauty was one of their star searchers, rescuing 63 other animals. After the War, in 1945, she was awarded the Dickin Medal.

Animals continue to be used in emergencies and times of conflict. The giant Gambian pouched rat has been trained to trace anti-personnel mines in Middle-Eastern trouble spots and dolphins are used to locate underwater mines. On September 11th 2001, an infamous date, Roselle, a Labrador guide-dog, led her owner to safety from the 78th floor of the Twin Towers in New York. As a gesture to all the more than 300 search and rescue dogs of the New York Police's K9 Department, a Dickin medal was presented to one of their number, Appollo. They all deserved it.

Tributes can take other forms, also. The British model-maker, Corgi, recently made a limited edition of the Spitfire airplane flown by one of the air aces of the Battle of Britain which took place between British and German forces in the skies above southern England from the 10th July-31st October 1941. Not only did the makers commemorate the pilot and the plane but they also included his dog, a German Shepherd called Flash which was the squadron mascot.

When the Norwegian ship '*Thorold*' was stationed in Scotland during the war, the ship's mascot, a St Bernard named Bamse became a favourite with the townsfolk. When the ship was in port, Bamse's duty was to round up the men who had gone into town: he would go into the bars of Montrose and collect the crew, herding them on to the dock. On one occasion he saved one Norwegian sailor when, in a drunken brawl, his opponent pulled a knife, by pushing the attacker into the sea. Bamse was sorely missed when he died in 1944, so much so that at his funeral almost 800 children who'd known and loved him, lined the route to say farewell.

Do visit the memorial in Park Lane and bear in mind what the inscription says, 'They had no choice', for as the Scottish philosopher David Hume said of our fellow animals, 'The question is not do they think, but do they feel?'